The Heart That Forgives

by Danielle N. Hall and Featured Forgivers

Copyright © 2023 by Danielle N. Hall

All scripture quotations are public domain courtesy of Bible Gateway: www.biblegateway.com

All Rights Reserved. No part of this publication may be reproduced, stored in a retrieval system, or transmitted in any form or by any means, electronic, mechanical, photocopying or otherwise, without the prior written permission of the copyright owner.

ISBN: 979-8-9869160-9-5

Cover Design, Editing & Typesetting by LaKesha L. Williams (www.coachkesha.com)

Published by The VTF Group LLC, Houston, TX
www.TheVTFGroup.com

ALL RIGHTS RESERVED | PRINTED IN THE USA

Table of Contents

Dedication	4
Acknowledgments	5
Foreword	10
Introduction	13

Stories of Forgiveness

Broken Little Girl by *Candis Scippio*	16
The Release by *Sheena Moton*	21
Out of Sight by *Danielle N. Hall*	32
Dear Me, I'm Sorry! by *DeVita J. Parke*	42
It's Not About You/It's About Me by *Eld. Terri Houston*	48
The Shirt Off My Back by *E. T. Armstrong*	58
The Journey by *E. T. Armstrong*	67
The Onion by *Janice Bennett*	72
Apology Denied by *LaKesha L. Williams*	79
Conclusion	95
Appendix A	97
Songs of Healing & Forgiveness	98
About the Author	99
Other books by the Author	100
About the Publisher	101

Dedication

This collaborative work is dedicated to every yielded vessel of the Lord, who has allowed His Spirit to be in control and guide him/her through the process of forgiveness. You made a significant life decision to set both your offenders and yourself free!

Acknowledgements

To My Heavenly Father
Before I can acknowledge anyone, I owe my first expression to my Heavenly Father. There is no way to write anything about forgiveness without having to give it and being open to receive it. The love from the Father has transformed my life in a way that causes me to truly love without conditions. The turning point in my life regarding forgiveness was when in 2002 a minister said to me these simple, yet profound words: *"God has already forgiven you, you just haven't forgiven yourself."* In that moment I experienced Your love and I have a greater capacity to both love and forgive. I am able to love beyond the offenses and to forgive for the offenses. I've also been granted the divine wisdom to know and understand that while we are required to forgive, we are not required to maintain unhealthy relationships. The best relationship to fully focus on is our relationship with You. All else comes after. Thank You for Your unfailing love, Your forgiveness of my sins of both commission and omission, and Your dispensation of wisdom and grace that allow me to successfully navigate through this life.

To My Late Parents in Heaven
Robert Henry Brock-Smith, Sr. & Cheryl Vanessa Brock-Smith the life, the lessons, and the love you gave me will forever be cherished. By demonstrating, you taught me what selflessness and service look like. I cannot fully express how much your physical presence is missed, but I'm constantly reminded by God that you are very much present. It is my endeavor to honor your life and cherish precious memories as long as I have breath. Without you, there would be no me. I never felt unwanted, and I consistently felt supported: from elementary school assemblies

and spelling bees, to growing up and birthing children of my own, and to my life in ministry. You've sown into me with time, treasure, and words of affirmation. I know that if you were physically present, this project would make you proud. I'll simply smile at the thought. I miss you sorely, but I encourage you to continue to show up in the ways that you do to let me know that you've taken flight, but haven't abandoned me. Rest well, Black Squirrel & My Pearl.

To My Children
Jayla, Maurice, and Aaron you all share me with the world. Being children of a visionary can be a challenge, because there is always something going on. You all show your support by listening, encouraging me to rest when it's clear I need it, preparing and serving me meals, doing my laundry, and even offering advice. You do those things from your heart, and it doesn't go unnoticed or under appreciated. I pray that as I have had the privilege to glean from the example of my parents, you will have gleaned much from me by my life lived out loud. You all are visionaries in your own right and I look forward to what you will share with the world as God leads you. I love you all to life!

To the Authors
Candis, my dear cousin-sister…we have been like peas in a pod since our Sq___ and Sq_____ days! (Insider lol) We have shared many experiences: some heartwarming, some heartbreaking, and some hilarious. The bond we share is pure and I enjoy our moments of laughter so much. To have you share in this experience means more to me than you know. I know it wasn't easy, but the ice is now broken, and I look forward to YOUR book. Yep, I said it…there is more. This is just the beginning.

The lives that you will impact with your unadulterated truth is more than you'll be able to count. In the words of the great Thomas Dexter Jakes: "Get ready, get ready, get ready!!!" I love you, Healed Woman!

DeVita, God knew exactly what He was doing when He put the fire in my life. You keep me on my toes and in my Word: which is a GREAT asset to our sisterhood/friendship. I would not trade it for the world. The consistent AHA moments we have with God are things I look forward to regularly. When God is in it, you are with it, and I thank you for both trusting the God in me and giving your yes. Your journey to forgiveness and passion regarding forgiveness is life changing and I thank you for sharing a piece of it here. Love you, Bird!

Elliott, writing is not something foreign to you. I've seen the work of your pen and how you take the reader on a journey. Your creative way of expressing yourself will reach audiences you have not dreamed of. To have you as a part of this experience is considered nothing short of a blessing. Though you are the only male participant in this project, what you have to offer is just as meaningful as you giving the shirt off your back. Thank you for thinking it not robbery to be a part of this necessary work. May your story set captives free. MUCH love to you, E.T.!

Janice, peeling back the layers would find itself being a challenging, but not impossible task. Your "yes" was easy, but I know that the work after the yes was a little intimidating. Just like the overcomer that you are, you rose to the occasion, grabbed the assignment by the horns, and brought it down. Your authenticity is just one of the reasons why I admire you and appreciate you. Your willingness to surrender to being naked will break the chains off shackled hearts and minds and will shatter fetters. Thank you for the yes and the yield. Love ya, Gift!

Sheena, I have known you for six years now and we have had the joy and pleasure of writing together, but also sharing many God moments whenever we converse. It's a thing that cannot be explained, it can only be experienced. I'm grateful for those moments and to also share in the writing experience together again. From the My Whole Self Matters Empowerment Journey Journal to My Praise is My Weapon, to our phone and in-person conversations: we have had some stories to tell. Thank you for releasing your heart on forgiveness here. I am grateful. Love you, Sis!

Terri, I am so honored that you joined us. That truly is putting it lightly. You being willing to share your raw, but relatable truth touches my heart deeply and I'm sure it will do the same for others. You are a leader in various capacities and a woman who wears many hats. May those within your reach see the Light shining through you and be led to their own path of forgiveness: even if it is having to forgive themselves. Blessings & Love, Sis!

To the Author of the Foreword
Vanessa, you have been a consistent force in my life for the majority of my years. I can think of countless conversations and many classroom lessons. I've not known you to be at a loss for words or anything less than articulate. When I was reminded of the other key parts of a book besides the chapters, ONLY your name came to mind regarding the foreword. I knew it would be in good hands. You proved me right. Thank you for saying yes

without hesitation, but thank you mostly for still being an intricate part of my life. I am exceedingly grateful and glad. Love you to life!

To the Publisher
LaKesha, it feels like I've known you for a lifetime, but it's only been seven years and we have accomplished MUCH together. You have handled my "babies" with care each time and have made the process easy to navigate through each time. My first writing experience with you was being a part of your baby: Hope for the Overcomers Soul. Ever since that experience, I have not hesitated to utilize the Vision to Fruition services for my books. This project is certainly stepping into another space. I'm grateful that you not only accepted the opportunity to serve in the publishing capacity again, but you have even joined in the number of contributing authors. You didn't just join, though: you came out with the big guns, and I am not mad at ya! THANK YOU SO MUCH! You may be the publisher, but I'm grateful to call you friend. Love you much, LaKesha! (In my Siri voice lol)

Thank you all!

Foreword

*I*n the book of Jeremiah, there's a statement that makes you wonder if there's any hope for human beings when it comes to virtues like forgiveness.

Are we even wired to forgive? If we genuinely do, is it the rule or the exception? Can it be taught? Is forgiveness one of those things in life we shouldn't expect, but should be grateful to receive? Jeremiah 17:9 (KJV) reads: *"The heart is deceitful above all things, and desperately wicked: who can know it?"*

As much as we declare our feelings, and often emphasize them by uttering *"with all my heart,"* or *"from my heart,"* or even *"from the bottom of my heart,"* (and that's deep), how much can we trust the sincerity, or believe the integrity of anything emanating from a place that's deemed, not just wicked, but *"desperately wicked?"*

The prophet didn't make any exceptions. He said THE heart. That indicts us all.

Is hearing *"I forgive you,"* then, an anomaly? A shock? A relief? Is it unusual? Is it a manipulative, or guilt inspiring utterance, or one that is full of liberty and love for the speaker and the recipient? Is *"I forgive you"* a treasure that inspires us to gladly reciprocate compassion and understanding when the opportunity arises?

I've known the individual behind this gathering of essays ever since she was in third grade. From that day to this, she has been kind, helpful, generous, long suffering, encouraging, and honest.

I can say all of that based on what I've observed. She's just about one of the nicest people I've ever met! Surely, Jeremiah didn't mean her! I'm pretty sure I've said that I can *"see"* her heart. But can I? Do I know it the way, perhaps, her late parents did? Do I see what her siblings or children see? Further, do I know her heart like God does? I've often wondered how does someone like her—anyone—who's experienced pain, loss, grief, mistreatment, disappointment and all the other difficulties that this life surely brings, continue to extend grace, even to those who absolutely don't deserve it? How does the capacity to continue to engage and forgive not diminish, or disappear altogether? How does that *"nice"* person not abandon the pursuit of godliness, ignore conviction, and join the ranks of the cold, stubborn, hateful, and heartless? It's no easy feat, but it demands the ability to look at the big picture. That heart has to both be surrendered and undergo divine transformation. It has to be healed. It must be overtaken by the pure, genuine, unconditional love of God. A new narrative has to be etched on that heart— one that rejects the inclination to be a right fighter, to demand one's own way, or insist that one's own feelings prevail.

The heart that forgives is extraordinary, but not elusive. It desires to please and be like God. It doesn't surrender to the goading of those who are anxious to see a fight, or maintain strife, misunderstanding, and division. It daily rids itself of the natural, understandable urge to retaliate, hate, dismiss, judge, punish, and throw others away. A heart that forgives restores years, allows rest, cleanses thoughts, guides actions, fosters and preserves peace.

A heart that forgives is entirely possible—with God. You realize that it's Him—His Spirit, His will, and His reflection that you see in the countenances and actions of those who have chosen to do so.

"But this shall be the covenant that I will make with the house of Israel; After those days, saith the Lord, I will put my law in their inward parts, and write it in their hearts; and will be their God, and they shall be my people." - Jeremiah 31:33 (KJV)

Vanessa Renee Williams

Introduction

Sometimes, the heart is so heavy from being full of the issues of life. The weight of grief from loss, the weight of being a parent, the weight of being a caregiver, the weight of being a friend, the weight of being a sibling, the weight of being a child, the weight of being a spouse, the weight of being single, the weight of being divorced, the weight of strained relationships, the weight of being a homeowner, the weight of being an employee, the weight of being an entrepreneur, the weight of ministry, or even the weight of news of current events can put a strain on the heart. Our lives are saturated with responsibilities, and it can sometimes seem like there aren't enough hours in a day or there isn't strength to grab a hold to. We then find ourselves engaging in unhealthy habits like resorting to fast food, eating late, turning to destructive vices, or not getting enough rest. We are exhausted mentally, physically, and emotionally. Chances are, we don't have time to read our Word, so we become undernourished spiritually. Our hearts are on overload, and it starts to manifest. Our patience begins to run thin and our words become less kind. We are ultimately agitated because of the weight. Physically, a heart that is overloaded can cease to work and that weight we carry can become a slow and silent killer.

When we fail to forgive, we can experience a similar consequence. Having lack of forgiveness in the heart is weighty and has a domino effect. The truth is that lack of forgiveness is a sin and sin can cause sickness. As a matter of fact, the wages of sin is death. We have this gift offered by God, though. Romans 6:23 (AMP) reads: *"For the wages of sin is death, but the free gift of God [that is, His remarkable, overwhelming gift of grace to believers] is eternal life in Christ Jesus our Lord."*

We are the offspring of a gracious, loving, and forgiving God. He's the God who made the ultimate sacrifice for us: not because we deserved it, but because He loved us so. Agape, or God's love, is unconditional and does not keep offense. God sent His ONLY begotten Son to die for a people who didn't deserve it, just so we might have life and have it more abundantly. When we fully receive this gift, our hearts ought to be cleansed and renewed. We cannot afford to hold on to offenses. Sometimes, we forget that we have been in the position of offender. How can we have the audacity to not forgive when the Lord laid down His life as a debt forgiveness gesture for us all? A lot of us profess to be Christians, but do we truly follow His example? When Jesus walked the Earth, He both taught and demonstrated what our surrendered lives should look like. When His disciples asked Him to teach them to pray, the response was as follows: *"He said to them, "When you pray, say: 'Father, hallowed be Your name. Your kingdom come. 'Give us each day our daily bread. 'And forgive us our sins, For we ourselves also forgive everyone who is indebted to us [who has offended or wronged us]. And lead us not into temptation [but rescue us from evil].'"* (Luke 11:2-4 AMP)

To receive forgiveness, we must first forgive and refuse to hold on to the wrongs we have experienced. If not, the stench of lack of forgiveness begins to seep from our hearts into our words and interactions. It begins to become toxic and while it is slowly killing us, it also kills relationships that should otherwise be maintained.

In the pages to follow, you will find that we all have a story and sometimes that story includes unfair and hurtful experiences. Sometimes, the experiences are results of our own choices and the person we need to forgive is self. You may see yourself in these accounts, but the beauty in each of them is forgiveness has been applied so debts have been cancelled. Just like when Jesus died on the cross and cancelled ours. May you be inspired by the words in the pages to follow from the hearts of those who have forgiven.

Danielle N. Hall

"Broken Little Girl"

Candis Scippio

When we are first born, we are as close to perfection as humanly possible. We have not yet committed our first act of sin. In so many words, we are whole. We know no wrong, no fear, no disappointment. However, in short order we begin to learn what all these things are, by way of our own experiences. For some of us, those experiences are too much for our little child minds to bear. As a coping mechanism, the mind begins to splinter, compartmentalize, and become desensitized to certain emotions. We become broken. Now from the outside, some faint cracks may show, but the true damage is not readily detected. That's because little girls learn very quickly how to camouflage. Through the untrained eye, all seems to be well. She seems to have found friends, she keeps up with the latest trends, she gets on her parents' nerves like everyone else. But underneath she is searching, and she doesn't know what for and she doesn't know where it is. So, she looks under every rock, behind every bush, in back alleys behind dumpsters, in school bathrooms, in her friends' houses, in trusted adults...she looks everywhere. And many times, she thinks she may have found it, but later discovers--sometimes after life-altering decisions--that wasn't it either.

You may find yourself somewhere in her, but this character study is of me. I was broken. After multiple compound fractures, the little girl inside me died, but I couldn't tell anyone. When I showed up, they expected to see her. No one bothered to notice the cracks and I was angry about it. I was bitter, resentful, and despondent. I didn't think anyone ever loved me or ever would. I began to morph into different characters depending on who I was interacting with, just to be *"accepted"*, but one can only pretend for so long, and when the real me showed up they didn't want any parts of it.

You may be wondering, *"I thought this was supposed to be about forgiveness."* It is. Let me explain. Because of all I went through and the subsequent choices I made as a result, I thought I had to forgive the absentee, alcoholic father, who never showed or taught me how to love myself. I thought I had to forgive the mother, who brought in a father figure, only for him to repeatedly abuse me, because she didn't have the strength enough at the time to let him go. I had forgiven them all and yet still felt some kind of way. That's when I knew I had to forgive God.

Yep, I said what I said. I didn't want to admit it, but I was angry with God; because my whole life all I heard was how good God is and how loving and kind and merciful He is. I remember being a wee little thing sitting up in church with Grandma, amazed at the whole experience. I could feel His presence even then. So why did He let me go through so much pain at such a young age and then for so many years thereafter? Why didn't He protect me? Why didn't He punish those who hurt me? Why didn't He show me who the bad people were? I didn't understand it and I was afraid to admit being angry at God but deep down, I knew I was.

When I was finally ready to face it, I first repented, then I told God that I was releasing Him of the blame for everything that went wrong in my life. I apologized for rejecting Him because of this secret blame. I was preaching, teaching, and shouting-- which could not have been real because I was angry with Him-- so I apologized for playing church and thanked Him for His mercy toward me by not striking me down where I stood. Then I forgave myself for being so stubborn and for wallowing in that mess for so long, acting like everything was okay. He never needed my forgiveness, because He had done nothing wrong—this was so I could get free. God deals in truth, and the truth shall make us free.

My journey from whole infant, to broken little girl, to broken young woman, to whole grown woman has been filled with twists and turns, and I know it's not over yet…but facing the truth and dealing with it allowed me to let go of all the pain from those fractures and let them heal, thus opening my heart to receive God's love. Do I have it all together now? Of course not! But I am better than I was. If you are upset with God, it's time to release it. You have so much life left to live, to be enjoyed, to be shared. There are people waiting to receive something only you can give them. He knows you're mad, but He still loves you! He never left you. He's waiting for you. It's time. John 5:6 KJV: *When Jesus saw him lie, and knew that he had been now a long time in that case, he saith unto him, Wilt thou be made whole?*

Candis Scippio

Candis Scippio is an ordained reverend, loving mother, and proud grandmother. Known for her ability to connect with people from all walks of life, Candis encourages those around her and inspires them to embrace their own unique paths of purpose and service. Candis takes great joy in being a doting grandmother. She cherishes the precious moments spent with her granddaughter, imparting wisdom and love and creating lasting memories.

Candis has always been passionate about writing; drafting poems, plays, and songs from her early childhood. She uses it to get herself through challenging times, and now hopes her words will help others do the same. Candis lives a life driven by love, faith, spiritual calling, and a deep desire to make a positive difference.

The Release

Sheena Moton

All my life, I have strived to make the best out of it. I have experienced deep hurts. I have been betrayed and cheated on, I have been a victim of crimes: theft and vandalism of both vehicles and personal property. I have been sexually abused as a child. I've experienced the loss of family members because they were murdered. I have been physically & verbally abused as a teen into adulthood. I have been lied to and on. During those times the only thing I could focus on was how the pain of those experiences and deep hurt made me feel, how they affected various relationships, and how I suffered from the memories of certain places and the things that were around when those deep hurts occurred.

There was so much hurt around me at one point, I just could not stop the pain. It began to affect me physically and spiritually. I had a co-worker that was very dear to me, and she said to me one day, *"I know you are tired of going through this sickness and pain. I have this new drug hot on the market, and I think you should try it. A lot of people say that it makes you love everybody, it opens you up to compassion, it heals deep wounds, it makes you even lose the weight you are carrying"*. I looked her in the eyes and said I am sold on the weight part. How do I get this drug? What is the name of it? She leaned in close and whispered: *"It's called FORGIVENESS. It's a strong medicine and it is not in generic form."* I just looked at her with the "YOU *GOT ME"* face, but I understood what she was saying to me and the answer was not at that point. I had not tried forgiveness, but I am ready to try anything to get rid of this pain. This was back in 2009.

Over the years I have learned that taking doses of forgiveness cures everything. My Pastors at VCMI-Suitland have often preached about the healing virtue in forgiveness. So, I have been learning a thing or two since taking my new prescription. This forgiveness prescription has amazing side effects. Forgiveness has allowed me to be stress-free. It has removed me from anger and hostility and it ultimately allows me to be FREE...free to BE Sheena. Additionally, there are extra benefits in freeness that forgiveness gives. It's all included in a few other components. These components are a part of the process. You must be willing to learn those components for yourself. What I have learned is that God forgives me, His love won't let me suffer, I don't have to be in bondage or be in victim mode. God wants to help all of his children and heal us from the past. Let's rejoice in the benefits forgiveness brings.

As I approached my 46th birthday, it did not take me long to realize that investments are associated with forgiveness. There is a cost to forgiveness that I never even considered. You were probably asking what do investments have to do with forgiveness? I said the same thing until God showed me what I was investing—the investment of emotions, mental and physical energy, and monetary items was the start of it. I will even add blood, sweat, and tears to the mix and because I stayed focused on the investment that I was putting in; it made the choice of letting go more difficult. In all actuality, there are many reasons why we experience these difficulties. God never said this road would be easy. Forgiveness includes acknowledging the hurts of the past, grievances, and regrets.

True forgiveness requires no condemnation so that means when you forgive, you forgive for real...not forgiving with conditions.

Some people say "I will forgive, but I will never forget". Well, that is not true forgiveness: sorry, but not sorry. One who forgives completely does just that - they forgive COMPLETELY. Think about our Father in heaven. What if He said He would only forgive us a little bit and day by day throw things back up in our face? How would that make you feel? You would probably feel pretty low, unworthy, unforgivable, and not chosen. Have you ever felt that way? To be honest, I surely have and more than once. We all want to be forgiven. We also need to understand the path that God has for us, even in forgiveness. We need to understand the benefits of forgiveness. God wants us to know that forgiving is a really big deal. In spite of everything mentioned above, Forgiveness is an investment like no other.

I am God's chosen vessel! I am God's favored! I am God's beloved! The devil wanted nothing better than for me to hold on tight to bitterness, resentment, envy, malice, self-doubt, self-sabotage, and thinking about self, self, self, self, self. He wanted nothing better than to have me focus on myself, other people, and worldly pains. All of these areas are a part of unforgiveness. See in John 10:10 KJV the bible says: *The thief cometh not, but for to steal, and to kill, and to destroy: I am come that they might have life, and that they might have it more abundantly.* I was focused on the beginning part of that scripture, but through the years I learned that God is telling us what the devil comes to do so we can be prepared. It is also for us to know what God comes to do and that He trumps what the devil had planned. God gives us an abundant life. So, I have to not hold onto unforgiveness. Unforgiveness is nothing but a big distraction.

Our instructions for life are in the Word of God. As a part of my healing journey, I had to discover deeply my identity in Christ.

I had to learn to no longer hold on to what the enemy had for me. It was time to make an exchange, let go of the unforgiveness, hold on to God's unchanging hand and see what it looked like to trust God in every area of my life. God was preparing my training grounds and cross-over all at the same time. After all of that I do JUST trust God! He wants the best for me and for you. I became fond of the scripture in the way The Passion Translation describes it in Jeremiah chapter 29. In verses 11-13, it states: *I know what I'm doing. I have it all planned out - plans to take care of you, not abandon you, plans to give you the future you hope for. "When you call on me, when you come and pray to me, I'll listen. "When you come looking for me, you'll find me.* Here you will see that God is the only One who knows the plans for your life. He knows what's good for you because He created you.

I remind myself that I am God's creation. I was created in His image, and in His likeness. I remind myself that God is ordering my steps. He has a purpose and a plan just for me. I know there is something more to forgiveness that God wants me to do. I just don't know exactly what it is as of yet. As my relationship gets closer with God, I began to ask Him how forgiveness ties into my purpose. One day I was at a tent revival in Downtown DC with my best friend (She is my Jonathan, and I am her David) and at the end of the revival session that night, a young girl came up to me and said: "Whoever said that curiosity killed the cat is a liar and they must return to the pits of hell. God loves your curiosity Sheena and wants you to ask Him even more questions because He has all the answers".

You didn't have to tell me twice, as my mom says. I began to ask God more and more questions. I really was seeking His answers.

I did not get all the answers to the questions right away, but God indeed took me on a journey. God took me out of my own state to a conference in Florida in 2022 and that started the revealing process to those questions. That round-trip ride to Florida and back to Maryland was more than I could ever ask for. But again, God said he loved my curiosity. You might be wondering what questions did I ask of God? Well, here is a snapshot into a few of them.

1. God, can You please show me who the people are that I have yet to forgive?
2. God, can You please show me the people who I need to ask forgiveness from?
3. God, can You please show me what Your forgiveness looks like toward others?
4. God, can You please show me how to reflect on Your scriptures on forgiveness?
5. God, can You please show me how to let go of the hurt and pain?
6. God, can You please show me how I can maintain forgiveness?
7. God, can You please show me how to pray for the person who hurt me?

And then I asked God ...

8. Could He please show me how to break completely free?

All the questions were answered for sure. The last question's answer was spoken towards the end of the conference. God spoke in a message that I knew was exactly for me. In that message I heard the following words that would change my life: *Pop,*

Release, Now! I was so excited in so many ways. For one, my last question was number 8. The number 8 symbolizes *"New Beginnings"* and the second part is that God said it and I believed it. I could see it, hear it and feel it…The Release! Letting go of something can be a very difficult thing to do, but when God tells you to do it, you must listen and obey.

On October 14, 2022, I was standing in the middle of a hotel lobby in Woodbridge, VA when God spoke to me. He promised me that he would give me enough grace for the Release. He said that it was time to let go of people places and things. Because I have begun the healing process and started to walk in forgiveness, that everything would not go into my next. God also said that I would need to be open to receiving the new people, places, and things He had for me, but yet there still had to be a release.

I had to learn how to let go of things that had me bound and learn how to let go of things that no longer served purpose in my life. God said that the release is a part of forgiveness that I had yet to master even though I had taken the test many times. I would let go and then take it back. I have been called to Reign like never before and there are things that are required of me in this season of my life as God elevates me higher. It will require me to embrace The Release.

The word release, by definition as a verb, is best described as allowing or enabling one to escape from confinement or be set free. As a noun, it is defined as the action or process of releasing or being released (www.dictionary.com). In general, release to me is defined as when someone or something is no longer confined or in prison, no more in bondage: there is no more confinement or being cooped up, there is no more obligation or pain, there is no longer being a hostage or restrained.

To release is also likened to a catapult. I had a vision of a blue catapult once. God showed me that He was placing us in the catapult one by one and releasing us into our destinies. The release helps to lose, to deliver, to extricate, and to disengage. God desires that after we walk in forgiveness we are no longer imprisoned or confined, and we are free from anything because what occurred is now out in the open with God and the enemy can no longer use it to torment or to hinder us. The release is FREEDOM and that is one of the components that occurs after forgiveness.

God wants us to be free! He said in His Word that whom the Son sets free is free indeed, so in this chapter God wanted me to share with each of you about "The Release". Wow, release is a really strong word. I never took time to think of just how powerful it is. It is the forgiveness that makes the release real. It's in the release that you can heal.

The release is real. Now it's time to put it into action. Create your very own "Release Strategy," here is mine. Feel free to add to it or change it around. Make it a part of your declaration of release.

- Allow God to lead you into how, who and what to release from: by His grace and by His Spirit He will do it.
- Allow your life to always be filled with JOY: joy that the world can't give, and the world can't take away.
- Understand that every time you don't forgive and release, you are placing yourself back in captivity.

- The release is helping you in your relationship not religion-ship with God. Listen to and obey God when He tells you how, who, and what to release.
- Apply the Word of God to your life daily.
- PRAY without ceasing.
- PRACTICE LETTING GO! Embrace it.
- REPEAT-THE RELEASE.

Sheena Moton

SHEENA MOTON, CEO/Founder of New Birth and Breathe Kingdom Services whose primary focus is to serve women in ministry; to help birth out their kingdom business visions. She is also an Evangelist who loves to share the good news of Jesus Christ with everyone she comes in contact with. She is an OVERCOMER, by the blood of Jesus and by the word of her testimony (Rev. 12:11). She is blessed to be a daughter of the King, His warrior princess, here on earth as it is in heaven. God has blessed her with ministries such as My WHOLE SELF Matters (helping women who have experienced trauma, abuse, and/or health challenges) and #RefreshHER (supporting new or seasoned women in ministry and servant leadership roles). Through both ministries, God has allowed her to disciple, love on, and encourage others. Standing on Jeremiah 17:14 (ESV) and Matthew 11:28-30 (NLT)

Sheena is currently pursuing a Bachelor of Arts Degree in Religious Studies from Victory Bible College (VBC) in Suitland, MD, graduating class of 2023 "The Fearless Ones". She leads with God's heart at Victory Christian Ministries International in the Children's and Fisher's of Men Ministries as an administrative coordinator; on the prayer ministry as an intercessory prayer leader, and was newly selected to serve Deacon. Sheena is committed with love to serving for the glory of God.

With over 20 years of experience, Sheena serves as a skilled workforce and family development specialist. She passionately works with homeless families under the District of Columbia's Family Rehousing and Stabilization Program and works with domestic violence organizations. Sheena proudly serves as a Liaison for Health & Human Services in the District of Columbia; Treasurer/Interim Secretary for The JC Pringle Foundation, Jonathan & Cheketa Pringle, Founders and most recently Ministry Assistant/Armor Bearer for the ministry of Prophetess Sherilyn M. Bennett.

Sheena adores her family. She is committed to the ministry of marriage with her husband of 20 years-Ramon Moton and is a mother of 5 daunting boys residing in the DMV area. They worship under the amazing leadership of Apostles Tony &

Cynthia Brazelton; Victory Christian Ministries International "One church in many locations" www.vcmi.org .

Connect with Sheena via email at mywholeselfmatters@gmail.com. You can follow the mission on the following social media platforms FB/IG @mywholeselfmatters.
From this ministry she is the Compiling Author of two books, "My WHOLE SELF Matters; Empowerment Journey Journal" and "My Praise is My Weapon" both currently available on Amazon!
"We are always seeking Ambassadors for Christ!"
2 Cor. 5:20
We are therefore Christ's ambassadors, as though God were making his appeal through us. We implore you on Christ's behalf: Be reconciled to God.
-Sheena Moton

Out of Sight

Danielle N. Hall

As a person whose eyes are almost always open looking for a sign or message from God, I see and process much on any given day. While traveling on the highway and local roads I find myself looking at messages on vehicles, looking at license plates, and making note of certain street names. When I was a young child, we'd often play the alphabet game where you'd look for the letters of the alphabet and call them out in order as you see them. The object is to be the first to complete all 26 letters. It seems easy enough, but unless you've played it you don't know how tough finding a Q can be sometimes. Another childhood memory is of a game show called Bumper Stumpers that used to come on the game show network. You had to try to figure out what the license plate was saying. My eye was trained at a very young age to look for patterns and figure stuff out.

Now in my years of spiritual maturity, I still look for patterns and make other observations, but I understand them on a different level. I almost always get excited when I see butterflies, they mean much to me. I personally identify with the butterfly because I know what it's like having been in a low place where I was vulnerable, just like the caterpillar. Yet, I found myself in hiding, became undone and broke free as a new creature. Did you know that once a caterpillar wraps itself in a cocoon or molts into a chrysalis, a radical transformation takes place on the inside. It's a work that is happening, but not in plain sight. The caterpillar digests itself and becomes like a soupy structure inside. There are then cells that multiply at the appropriate time forming the new creation that emerges at the appointed time. What a wonder! Again, it is something I personally relate to being regenerated after becoming undone and then emerging as something new in God's timing.

As captivating as butterflies are, I have found myself really captivated by the numbers 5, 55, 555, and 1111. Let me go ahead and add 8 for new beginnings in there, too. I can't truly explain what it does, but I'll attempt. It sorta does for me what a few shots of espresso does for a coffee drinker at the top of the morning. The screenshots of the 5:55 and 11:11 times in my phone are near countless. They can be counted, but I don't find it necessary to do so. The number 5 is the number of grace and because I have learned to rely so heavily on grace, seeing 5 excites me. I'm drawn to numbers, and I know that there is significance to them. As much as I am drawn to the number 5, I cannot say that I have an affinity for the 5th month of the year. I mean, I do like the date 5/5, but outside of that, I don't have a real connection. Perhaps it could be because of not so pleasant things that occurred in my life in the month of May.

If I travel backwards, starting with the more recent unpleasant experience, the date would be May 2, 2021. On this date, I watched my husband pass away unexpectedly in our bedroom in the middle of the night. It was traumatizing to say the least, but I thank God for the grace to endure it. Seventeen years before then on the same date, my youngest brother was murdered. That was on May 2, 2004: while I was very pregnant with my youngest son who was born on July 30, 2004. These are just a couple of many close losses I've endured.

There was this other May date that became a bit of a thorn for me: May 9th. On that date in 2010, it began as a normal Sunday. We got up and got dressed to make our way to church. This particular day happened to be Mother's Day that year. Speaking of Mother's Day, let's park there for a moment. As I mentioned, I've experienced many losses. On January 28th of this year, my mother transitioned. I was her only child so you can imagine Mother's Day being a bit different this year. She had just recently moved into my home on July 4, 2022. It was a joy to wake up and see her smile in the morning and receive her good morning kiss on my right cheek. I have to admit, that I was spoiled…not a brat, but definitely spoiled. Even after having been married with children, my mother would still purchase things like deodorant, sanitary napkins, and all sorts of other essentials. While she was here living with the children and I in the house, there was no shortage of home cooked meals from her. She very often fried chicken, which was tasty, but I needed variety and she'd oblige. She also would launder my clothes and fold and hang them up. She did much to make it a home and while those deeds are missed, her presence is most missed. I have many memories to cherish and plenty of pictures depicting her signature smile. One thing for sure: she loved her baby, and that same love keeps me full and going. There's nothing like a mother's love.

On that note, I want to double back to that Mother's Day on May 9, 2010. After participating in church service, my children and I went to visit my mother at my parent's home. It's the home where the living room walls were filled with family pics, Redskins stuff, and my honor roll certificates. When I pulled up on the street, I noticed quite a shortage of parking spaces. That wasn't uncommon: especially on holidays. I did observe one nearby parking spot on the opposite side of the street. I commenced to park and let my children out on the sidewalk and told them to wait. I turned around to get something from the back seat and then I observed what I would describe as an eerie silence. I got out of the car and noticed that the eldest and youngest of my children were already on the other side of the street. I didn't see the middle child, who is my eldest son who I affectionately call Big Boy. I came around the back of my Blue Mirage Metallic Blue Toyota Sienna minivan and noticed Big Boy on the ground. He was somewhat seated with his legs somewhat extended. I was confused for a second about why he was sitting in the middle of the street. Then it dawned on me, and I asked him was he hit by a car. He affirmatively responded and I looked for the person responsible. However, there was no car in sight. I had no way of identifying the driver or the vehicle because both were out of sight.

By this time, my mother was outside her door and that was the extent of my visit with her on that Mother's Day. What I did next may not have been the best choice, but as a mom, all I could do was think fast. The thought of calling 911 didn't even cross my mind. The thought was to get my son to the nearest hospital ASAP. I picked my then 7-year-old son up and placed him in the seat behind my driver's seat and I proceeded to the nearest hospital.

Once in the treatment area, they cut his pants leg to view the injury and it was an apparent broken bone because there was deformity. My emotions were mixed. I was deeply concerned for my son, but extremely upset with the person who caused this injury. My son had to be transferred to Children's Hospital in Washington, DC. As we awaited an update from the medical staff, I was nervous and angry. Eventually, we reunited with him. They had put a cast on his leg, and it turns out that it was too tight. The next day they had to remove it. As they were removing it, the saw that was used had gotten down to the skin level and added a new injury to the injured leg. By this time, I'm fuming, and no pain medication would bring him relief: no morphine, ibuprofen or Tylenol 3 was effective. I'm observing him endure this pain and it makes me even angrier because I had no one specifically to blame.

The weeks progressed and Big Boy would require surgery to have nails placed in his legs from his knee to his ankle. The surgery was successful, and he came home with a cast that covered his entire leg and it covered his foot. Only his toes were exposed. Life for us became challenging, but the greatest challenge for me was trying to put my full attention on his recovery. I wanted the person who was responsible for this tragedy to pay the price. The time would come when Big Boy would have another surgery: this time it was to remove the nails that had been placed to stabilize his bones back in place. One of the things that helped to lessen the impact of the process is that his orthopedic surgeon was skillful, and kind and his name was Dr. Lovejoy.

His office address was 888 Bestgate Drive. Look at that: new beginnings and we went to the right place. Dr. Lovejoy was amazing and very reassuring, but a place in my heart truly detested the one who made us even have to come to know a Dr. Lovejoy. As my son recovered, I would sleep on the couch in the living room because he had to stay on that level of the house. Fortunately, we had a suitable piece of furniture for him to attempt to rest on. Trips to the bathroom were an adventure. He had a wheelchair, and we had a half bath on that same floor. Maneuvering to get him in the bathroom and then hurrying to get a folding chair and pillow for him to prop his foot up so blood wouldn't rush to the injury site was a task. Big Boy remained a trooper through it all. Because of his tenacity, I had to fight to be strong. I must say, though, just because that driver was out of sight, he wasn't out of mind. Every bit of suffering I observed my son go through was piercing to my heart. I didn't like the feeling at all.

Big Boy recovered well and would later sign up for the local football team. I can't say that I was thrilled, but he enjoyed the game. He played a couple of different positions and was handling his own on the field. I was still a nervous mom. The thought of my children being hurt remains a problem even now. Eventually, he moved on to another team. I could only make it through a couple of games because the weather was unseasonably warm which was not a good match for the vertigo I've battled since being a preteen. I recall overheating at one of his games and I was heading back to my car, but passed out at the gate. If you've never dealt with vertigo, then you're blessed. It is not an easy condition to deal with. I supported Big Boy how I could, but being outside at the games wasn't it.

On October 11, 2015, Big Boy sustained another injury that involved a break. This time it was on the football field at a game that took place before I had gotten out of church. I received a call from his father that pretty much said they were on the way to the hospital and to meet them there. I was fuming just as when he was the victim of the hit and run. This was another hit that caused him an injury in football, but it was by a bigger guy, and it was a dirty play. It was an intentional attempt to hurt him. This time Big Boy's wrist was broken, and the break was through his growth plate. Again, we are in the emergency room with him suffering from an injury inflicted by whom I would then refer to as cowards. There was no way I could have him go back on the field to play again. My heart couldn't take it. Something happened though, as he lay there on the stretcher with his hand dangling from some antiquated contraption, he adamantly expressed wanting to play again. He said something, though, that blew my mind and caused me to pause. He said something to the extent of *"If I could overcome a car, what's a person?"* In other words, Big Boy had no fear in spite of these unfortunate injuries he sustained. At no point did he express to me a hatred or strong negative feeling for the driver who hit him or the football player.

Isaiah 11:6 says: *"...and a little child shall lead them"*. This young man who experienced the hit and run at 7, and then the football hit a couple of months before turning 13, was indirectly leading me to the right mindset. There was no held grudge. The focus was on recovery and return. How many times do we focus on an offense? How many times have we found ourselves in a place of unforgiveness because we don't think the person is worthy or receiving said forgiveness? God has a way of getting our attention. In this case, He was getting my attention through my son's example. Both of the offenders were out of sight, and I was harboring unforgiveness in my heart for people I couldn't identify.

A Mark Twain quote is *"Forgiveness is the fragrance that the violet sheds on the heel that crushed it."* Mahatma Ghandi said *"The weak can never forgive. Forgiveness is the attribute of the strong."* In Mark 11:25-26 (KJV) Jesus said: *"And when ye stand praying, forgive, if ye have ought against any: that your Father also which is in heaven may forgive you your trespasses. But if ye do not forgive, neither will your Father which is in heaven forgive your trespasses."* As one who was committed to serving the Lord and who had an active prayer life, to not forgive would've been both hypocritical and unwise for me. I thank God for the way He used my son to make me reflect on the words of His only begotten Son. God knows I've had thoughts, uttered some words and committed some deeds that required forgiveness. Who was I to deem anyone unworthy of the same grace. There may be some I have offended unbeknownst to me. There are a few that I know I have, even if that wasn't the intent. The point is we all have said, thought or done something that was unfavorable and frowned upon by God. Yet, He has been merciful and kind towards us and has forgiven even the things we have done that others have deemed as unforgivable.

Life has dealt me an interesting deck and I have had to forgive much, but I dare not deny someone a grace that I have received. Harboring unforgiveness can lead to a shackled heart and a miserable life. Christ died for all. He came to set the captives free. I'm not into bondage, so I refuse to allow any out of sight or identifiable offender to rob me another moment of the gift of this freedom. Finally, in the words of Lewis B. Smedes: *"To forgive is to set a prisoner free and discover that the prisoner was you."*

Danielle N. Hall

Danielle N. Hall is a Board Certified Christian Counselor and Mental Health Coach who is an advocate for all to recognize and achieve their divine purpose. Additionally, is a licensed minister who is continually looking for ways to enlighten, to encourage, and to empower others through this journey called life.

She is a sexual abuse survivor and the visionary/founder of V.O.I.C.E. (Victorious Overcomers Inspiring Christian Empowerment) which is a ministry that services women who have been sexually assaulted or abused. She is the sole author of her debut book "Dew Drops: Refreshing for the Soul", her sophomore book: Amazon #1 Bestseller "Dirty Little Secrets & The Little White Lie."

and her junior release: Grace to Endure: You Don't Know My Story". Danielle has been a contributing author of 5 projects: She Wouldn't Let Me Fall (2018), Hope for the Overcomers Soul (2018), My Whole Self Matters Empowerment Journey Journal (2019), My Praise Is My Weapon (2020) and God Blocked It (2023).

She is a budding entrepreneur and is the owner of both SOL by Danielle (a greeting card service launched in 2017) and The Butterfly Effect by Danielle (a butterfly themed jewelry company launched in August 2019). In May 2023, Danielle launched The R.O.P.E., LLC (The Realm of Possibility Experience) where she will employ her skillset as a coach and counselor. She is a recently widowed mother of 3, who endeavors to both achieve and maintain balance given the demands of family, work, ministry, and self.

Dear Me, I'm Sorry!

DeVita J. Parke

Vita- I'm sorry for the hurt I've caused you. For leaving you to deal with the baggage of our past, alone. I'm sorry for numbing our pain with different men and food-causing you to bear a weight that was masked. I'm sorry for gossiping about others to take the attention from myself.

I'm sorry for allowing us to become pregnant at 14 and again at 16; this time causing you to have to make an adult decision when you were just a child. I'm sorry for convincing you that adoption was the only alternative. I'm sorry for not learning my lesson and becoming pregnant again-viciously repeating the cycle of creating love that we weren't prepared or responsible enough to care for. I'm sorry for listening to and allowing others to put you down and call you names: speaking word curses over you and our bloodline. I'm sorry for not speaking our truth when the molestation first occurred and for not sharing and exposing our predators. I'm sorry that when the main predator, Curtis, died I didn't allow you to forgive him or grieve for the only father you knew. I hated him and felt you did the same.

I'm sorry for pretending to be OK when, in reality, I was dying a slow death. I'm sorry for becoming and continuing to be emotionless.

I'm sorry that you felt unprotected, so much so, that you developed an uncontrollable temper that has nearly killed you.

I'm sorry, because I checked out, I never allowed you to check in: failing to give you the outlet you needed. I thought I was helping *you, but I was only helping our perpetrators continue to perpetuate our hurt-fuel our anger and intensify our fears.*

I'm sorry that before we could live, I tried to kill us. I'm sorry that I tried it several times over - I am thankful, that God kept us, though. But I'm sorry that I never allowed you to know GOD as a young girl.

I'm sorry that even now, when we see our predator William, I'm cordial to him. I'm sorry that I didn't teach you about forgiveness. I'm sorry that you feel that I've abandoned you; I didn't. See, I had to go through those things Vita, to become DeVita.

I'm sorry that you must watch me have a relationship with Dale, our mother, while you harbor the hatred that I once felt for her. I no longer feel hate for her. I now feel a great deal of sadness for her. Because no matter what, she will never be able to tell you she's sorry. She will never be able to regain your trust because she doesn't even know you.

I'm sorry that she will never know or understand the hurt she caused, by not loving herself enough to know she deserved more - In that, she would have a realized, we did too. But I do love her, I love her past her faults. Without her, Vita, we wouldn't be here. Too many times we blame people Vita for not growing up, and being who we need. But we too, will face that struggle. At one point in time, I wasn't who my children needed, but God! I am now!

I'm sorry that I was blinded by the idea of forgetting it all, that I forgot you too. I'm sorry that along the way, even when I became better I still had a thing for people using me, I even used a few in my time. I'm sorry for back peddling, for destroying things that were good, but cultivating the things that were bad.

I'm sorry that I paid too much attention to the things that just needed a glance. I'm sorry Vita, for teaching you to be sorry and instead of apologizing. Because Vita, there is a huge difference. Anything that comes after I am, defines you. We are NOT sorry, we were just a little girl who experienced more than what we should have in the lifetime, but as a woman, I now know, THIS was a part of God's design. I know you're still learning Vita, but it's true. And now, now that you've forgiven me...I'll teach you all the things you need to continue to heal and grow into the woman, God has called us to be. How you ask? We do by continuing to trust God, by allowing HIS will and not our own, to be done.

I'm sorry that I keep sharing our story, but each time that I do, I believe we're helping others like us. Which allows me to believe that God spared us to do just that. I know right now you don't understand that, but I do. I'll continue to teach you, until you're ready to be a part of me. Who I am today. You don't have to be scared anymore. The worst is over, the healing is just beginning....You don't have to be that little girl anymore. We have amazing people now who love us, who will do what's needed to protect us. If we allow it.

Vita, I apologize for not allowing you to meet and experience Delroy. I honestly didn't even expect to meet someone like him. Don't be so harsh towards him, although he's made mistakes, he's nothing like the men in our past.... He's a good man, who has made mistakes, but he too, has been hurt in life. I'm grateful that he's always praying to be better. He already is. Let's learn to give him a break, the grace/mercy that was extended to us, let's always extend it to him. This is why our healing is so important. Here's my hand, Vita. Grab it, we don't need to live through the open window, we can now come out and live beyond. We're free!

Vita, I'm sorry that you never met Elizabeth. Our God appointed mother. She was/is everything! She was the first person to see you and love on you. She opened my eyes to see that I couldn't be me without you.

Let's take it one day at a time. We'll fall, but we won't quit. We'll reach for one another, even when we don't feel like it, we will. We'll keep ourselves together. Knowing that God never left us, I did.

So, Vita, I apologize, and I promise to make it right. Please forgive me, because I forgive me-I'm no longer sorry!

I love you,
DeVita

DeVita J. Parke

DeVita J. Parke is a Maryland native and presently resides in Southern Maryland. She is a visionary, and it can be noticed through her works for the community as she strives to reach those by teaching the importance of forgiveness, healing and becoming who you have been purposed to be.

To date, DeVita is the Founder of 501c3 Non-Profit I Just Want 2 Help, Inc, Owner and Operator of Kupkaked by DeVita, President of ParkeD Enterprises and New Adventure Same Journey. DeVita is also a Board-Certified Christian Counselor. She shares her accomplishments with her children.

It's Not About You / It's About ME

Elder Terri Houston

People often tell me that they don't understand how I am not a grudge holder or how I can forgive those that have hurt me or tried to destroy me. I reply by referring to Colossians 3:13; *"You must forgive one another just as the Lord has forgiven you."* It's just that simple for me. Is it easy? NO!!! I have found during my journey that forgiveness is a powerful tool for the person able to forgive. It allows the person to let go of negative emotions: emotions like anger, resentment, and bitterness and then experience a sense of release and freedom. It reduces stress and promotes greater feelings of inner peace and well-being. I believe that forgiveness helps lift burdens and helps improve relationships. When one forgives, it helps us see the other person in a more positive light. It can help repair damaged relationships and maybe promote greater trust and intimacy. On the other hand, I feel that it is not necessary to continue a close relationship with the person. Actually, you don't have to have a relationship at all. But the feeling of peace and positive emotions that come with forgiveness is amazing.

My forgiveness journey started some 40 years ago. It started with me forgiving me. I believe forgiving yourself is the hardest. I was holding my self-forgiveness hostage.

At age 21, I was deeply depressed. I hated everything about ME and my life. So much so that I decided that Terri had no value and no place here. Now mind you, I was a single mother of a young child. Despite that fact, I decided to take a ride around the beltway after taking 48 extra strength Tylenol and drinking 40 ounces of malt liquor. At 3:00 am, I decided to park my car and walk to a nearby park. My plan was to lay in the grass, go to sleep and never wake up. Little did I know that GOD had other plans for me that night. I parked my car near a close friend's home. I could not believe that she was on her porch sweeping. THAT NIGHT CHANGED MY LIFE. My friend, realizing something was not right, took me to the hospital. The hospital was Catholic, but every meal a prayer was given and on every tray was Scripture. My roommate ended up being an older Baptist woman that insisted that I read the Bible with her every day. I resisted, but she kept pushing and eventually I gave in. When I think back to that time, I get chills. I thank God over and over for the plans that HE already mapped out for me.

I asked God to forgive me. I promised Him I would never attempt to take my life again. Because of the forgiveness that God gave me, I knew that I had to forgive anyone both now and in my future. I quickly realized that forgiveness gave me a sense of freedom and peace so that I could move in my life with joy and no regrets.

There have been many times in my life that I had to forgive and times that it meant asking to be forgiven as well. Sometimes, I really didn't feel like I should, I knew it was necessary. Asking for forgiveness can be extremely important in fixing a relationship or moving on. It's important that you address the fact that you have done something wrong or hurtful. If you care about continuing or repairing the relationship it will show the other person that you value them. In asking for forgiveness, you have to remember that the other person is not God and may not be willing or ready to forgive or not able to get past the hurt.

When this is the case, it is important that the other person's feelings are respected. Focus on learning from the experience, even if forgiveness is not granted.

As my journey continues, let's start with my first major moment. My 12th grade year, six months before graduation, I discovered that I was pregnant. I figured that I would graduate (I had to graduate after begging my parents to send me to a private school), marry the father, and live a great life. Of course, that was a dream.

So, there I was 18, pregnant, no job and a baby daddy. The first hurt was the night before my son was born, we had a big argument. He was with another woman. The second hurt, he came to visit and yet another argument. It was so bad, I started bleeding. He left. Then six weeks after giving birth to my son, I had to make a hard choice. Either I stay in a doomed, toxic, and unwilling relationship with my son's father or find a better life, a better alternative. Well, I chose the latter, MOVE ON!!! My son's father didn't even put up a fight, he just MOVED ON. I never tried to find him, never tried to obtain financial support. For 44 years, my son never knew his father. I was angry and hurt. But in those 44 years, I learned that in order to truly move on and give my son the best life that I could. I knew that FORGIVENESS would be necessary. I took responsibility for the part I played and forgave his father. Not one time did I speak bad of him. I only encouraged my son not to go through life waiting for his father to be a part of his life.

My son is now 46 years old and two years ago his father contacted us on social media. They have talked, but my son still has never met his father. Get this, we have traveled to North

Carolina three times since he contacted us. Only an hour away, and he has had an excuse not to meet us every time. Sometimes this angers me, and it all comes back, but I decided not to let the unforgiveness rise and continue to walk in forgiveness. We have conversations from time to time now. I'm asked how I can even want to talk with him. I believe that it's ok to be cordial and be respectful in this situation. Do I need him in my life, absolutely not. However, because I moved in forgiveness it was not hard for me to have a conversation with him. Do I want more, absolutely not.

No one has to understand or approve your forgiveness of someone or something. Move according to what God is telling you. The peace it gives is truly amazing. Forgiveness, for me is about freeing me of the tension and stress of constantly thinking about what was done wrong to me. It's not about letting that someone off the hook. It's not about continuing a relationship with them.

Continuing along this path of forgiveness, at age 25 I thought that I had found the love of my life. September 4th, 1984, that's the day. This roller coaster ride continues even today. This has been the hardest road of forgiveness for me. It has taken 39 years for me to be truly free.

For 11 years I lived with him, unmarried, and gave him my everything. Midway through I came home one night to an empty apartment and him waiting to say he was leaving. His father offered him a car to leave. I was crushed. And guess what, I had just found out that I was pregnant. I didn't want to tell him because you know the old saying: having a baby will make them stay. When I finally told him his parents convinced him that I was lying. I prayed every day that God would fix this once again mess of my life.

Then one Sunday, he decided that he wanted to attend church with me. While at church my prayer was answered, I miscarried, and he was there. Even with that I took him back and in 1995 I gave him an ultimatum; marry me or leave. He chose to marry!!! Today, I regret it. Now not every day was bad, don't get me wrong. There were some pretty good times. I was with the love of my life. The only problem, I don't think he was ever in love with me. Over the years it was more evident.

In 39 years, we have nothing. NO children, NO home, NO financial security. NOTHING and over the years my health started to decline. But I stayed. We tried counseling three times and each time I was asked, *"Minister/Elder what would God want you to do"*. Each time I listened and stayed because I was convinced that it was the right thing to do. We even renewed our vows after 10 years. Then in 2009, the ultimate betrayal. He decided he want to see if he could catch a *"younger, prettier woman."* The most hurtful part was, it happened with someone I knew. Someone that I had warned him about. I found out from a family member and soon found out a few friends and family knew because he bragged to them and of course when I confronted him, he denied it all.

The crazy thing is this came at a time when he was being considered for a deacon role and I had to be interviewed. So once again I gave him an ultimatum. You tell me the truth or tell Pastor the truth. He chose to tell me. So, from 2009 until 2016, once again I tried to continue with what I thought was the love of my life. I forgave him. Only this time, I fell out of love. My heart could not take any more disappointment and hurt. During these 7 seven years, I felt that I had forgiven him since I decided to hang in there. What I learned was my heart started hardening and my feelings became less and less. I asked God to show me how to forgive and heal myself. How do I forgive, but put myself first. Forgive and move on. How do I get peace in this situation and in my life. I wanted to be free.

From 2016 until the present, I have learned just that. I apologized for giving him the ultimatum because I knew he wasn't in love with me. I told him that I accepted my part in our failed relationship. I told him that I forgave him, but I was no longer in love with him. Of course, he automatically assumed that I must have been in love with another man because even our sexual relationship ended. NO, that was not it. I just wasn't in love with him and for me that is essential in an intimate relationship. I needed to guard my heart.

In the midst of this I had to once again put on my forgiveness hat and allow his elderly, sick father to move in with us: a man who helped him leave, a man that never wanted him to marry me…a man that I only felt empathy for, but never a father-in-law/daughter-in-law relationship. To me, he was Mr. Roberts. That's it, that's all. I was always kind to him and showed compassion, even when his son didn't: just at arm's length.

These past few years, I felt as though I was living in hell. So unhappy, no peace. Just determined not to get so depressed that I would go back on my promise to God. During the high moment of Covid I decided that I would not stay in a place of pain, unhappiness and no peace. I began walking every day. I had five other amazing ladies that walked with me. We all found healing and peace. I know for many Covid took a lot away, but for me it gave me a new life and I'm so grateful to God. Finally in October of 2022, I decided that if I was to have any peace in my life, I would have to leave. It was not easy and it was so scary, but I had to do it. One morning he woke up mean looking as usual and said that we might as well be divorced. I quietly said to him, please file if that will make you happy. That was my exit. I packed, put the unnecessary stuff in storage and took my necessities with me and left. It was necessary for ME. He says that I will never forgive him. I say I have forgiven him because the forgiveness was about me being free and moving on with my life and not trying to mend a relationship that will constantly need a band-aid. So here I am in a physical space to lay my head, that's not so comfortable and in a spiritual, soul – fulling place that gives me more peace than I have ever known and joy.

I have been hurt by so-called friends, business associates, family, and pastors. It continues. Even in these situations, I have acknowledged my part and forgave the other party. I remember writing a letter to a former pastor: someone who really taught me to have an authentic relationship with God and throw religion away. Our relationship ended on a bitter note. Then one day, GOD clearly spoke to me and said you must write him and ask for forgiveness in the part you played. I obeyed God. In the letter (which happened years after the issue) I apologized for my role in hurting our relationship and asked for his forgiveness. I thanked him for being a great pastor to me and that everything that I learned about really being a Christian came from his ministry. Months later I saw him at an event, and he came to me and said, *"I was about to give up my ministry. Then I found your letter buried under a pile of mail it bought me new hope and encouragement."* He thanked me. I thanked him. He's no longer with us, but that moment of forgiveness on both sides will always have an impact in my life.

I thank God every day for forgiveness and the freedom it provides from these relationships. For me it's not about forgetting what happened or excusing the behavior of the person that hurt me. It's about me being able to move on and heal from the wound. It has not been easy because in forgiving I remember and sometimes the anger and regret and resentment arise. I really had to make a decision to let go of the hurt and anger. It was hard, but necessary.

If Jesus could forgive those that tortured and persecuted Him and if God can forgive me every day for the wrong that I may do, then surely I can forgive those that hurt me. Surely, I can give grace when it's necessary. Most importantly, I deserve peace in my life. I deserve joy in my life. Forgiveness has allowed me to move away from anger, resentment, stress, hurt and depression and experience peace and joy beyond what anyone can imagine.

Elder Terri Houston Roberts, MBA

Visionary, Ordained Minister, Teacher, Mentor, Entrepreneur

As President and CFO of Roberts' Dynasty LLC, Terri H. Roberts started a business that would grow and build a dynasty for those coming behind her.

She believes that passion, purpose and destiny are the driving forces in being successful. Terri's number one passion is to be a motivator and inspire other women to reach greatness. To find their passion and purpose in order to get to their destiny.

Terri holds a Master of Business Administration from Trinity University with a focus on Non-Profit Management and Women Studies, Certifications in Advanced Project Management and Leadership, and Master Life Coach.

She is the owner of Roberts' Dynasty Tax Service, Yours Virtually, INC., Treasured Memories Events and Travel. She is an Ordained Elder. Following her passion and purpose to motivate and inspire other women of all ages, she recently took on the role as Vice President and CFO of Women Destined 4 Greatness.

She is a member of The Ministerial Alliance of Generation of Praise Christian Church, Girl Scouts of America, National Council of Negro Women, National Association of Tax Professional.

"Faith Over Fear, Service Over Self, Love over ALL!!!"

The Shirt Off My Back

E. T. Armstrong

I often tell people: *"I was a genius between kindergarten and the eighth grade."* I studied all the time, was timely with my schoolwork, and was eager to raise my hand to respond with the correct answers in class. I was often considered a nerd or that real smart kid. Females of different ages would say that I was cute, but no girl would talk to me. I will admit that I was shy and reserved. I was so in my mind that I would talk myself out of saying anything for fear of looking lame. I decided in the eighth grade that I would try my hand at sports.

When I was nine years old, I played recreational football, but because of my size I was moved up to the next age group. Those boys were bigger and had more experience. Turns out their size nor experience mattered because we lost every game. Consequently, I only played for one year. In the eighth grade they had try-outs for the football team, but someone told me they had a weight limit. I was 5'9" and weighed 165 lbs. Though I had thinned out, I was insecure about my size, so I didn't try out. When basketball season started, I decided to try out. To make a long story short, I didn't make the final cut. I spent the rest of the year practicing my passing and my shooting at home. I saw improvement, so I thought I'd try again.

At the end of the middle school year the high school across the street from my school posted a three-day try-out for a summer basketball camp for incoming freshmen. After school one day I walked over to the high school gym and tried out for the camp. I had improved my shooting ability, but I lacked the fundamentals of organized basketball. I was cut again. On the last day of the basketball camp tryouts, the head football coach came into the gym and invited us to an all-summer training for the football team that consisted of weight training, running and various football drills. I was the only incoming freshman out there working out with the team. The upperclassmen would always ask me why I was out there, and I told them: *"So I could get in shape,"* so they let it go. We worked out every day all summer until school started and I became a lot stronger, gained ten pounds, and grew three inches taller. It was our first full contact scrimmage with another team and the line coach (Coach Thomas) passed out random jerseys to players to wear during the game. I was invited and I wasn't sure if I would get in the game, but I was just glad to be part of the team.

On the bus, as we were traveling, the guys were trading their jerseys for their original numbers. I was the only freshman on the bus, and I had the star safety's number 42 (Chuck Ross). Chuck and his crew bullied and intimidated me the whole trip to the school because I had his jersey. I reluctantly gave him my jersey after he swore that he would give it back to me so I could turn it in. Chuck was an amazing football player, and I would see Chuck on the field from time to time, but halfway through the season, I was moved up to varsity, so I saw Chuck daily. I would always ask him about my jersey and, when I did, he would become irate and say: *"I told you I would give it back to you!"*. I figured that at the end of the season we all had to turn in our jerseys so it would be sorted out in the end.

Chuck was a highly recruited strong safety by many Division 1 schools, but his true ambition was to join the Marine Corp. His father was a Marine and that's all he talked about. When he graduated, he was going to enlist. Chuck was playing street football with some of his friends and shattered his ankle. His football season was over, but he still dressed out for the games on the sideline. The team needed him on the field playing and we desperately needed his participation. A few weeks later, at the end of the season, Chuck was informed that he would not be accepted into the Marines because of his ankle.

I woke up one day to get ready for school, I got dressed and walked to the bus stop. It was a foggy, rainy November morning and it just felt dreary. I got on the bus, and nobody was talking. I heard someone say: *"That is really messed up"* and I said: *"What is messed up?"* and that's when they told me that Chuck had died earlier that morning, and it was suspected that he shot himself.

In the middle of the night, Chuck had taken his father's rifle and walked into the woods. Chuck put the barrel to his neck and pulled the trigger. He left a note saying that his dream was to be a Marine like his father. He felt he had let himself and his family down and since he couldn't fulfill his dreams of becoming a Marine his life was not worth living.

When the bus arrived at school I got off and went to my homeroom. The principal (Mr. Riley) came on the intercom and announced the passing of Chuck earlier that morning. He explained that his family found his body and wanted to spread the news. It was hard to understand what Mr. Riley was saying because he was crying so hard. He announced that the office will be open for talking and consoling anyone that needed to talk. The counselors will be available throughout the day. The Head Coach (Coach Springs) called the whole team to the gym to speak with us and check on our status since we lost a brother. I went to the gym and sat on the bleachers while the coach talked about Chuck and how he was both a phenomenal player and a great person. I was thinking he was a bully: *"Big, Bad Chuck."*

A week later my mother took me to his funeral. I walked up front to view the body and he looked good, but he didn't have a neck. It looked like his head was just sitting on his shoulders and lying in his casket folded up nicely was my jersey. I can't fully describe how I felt seeing him there. I was shocked and a part of me wanted to reach in there and grab my jersey. I didn't want to make a scene. His family was going through enough and I knew that I would make a spectacle of myself, so I walked back and sat beside my mother and told her what I saw. I week later the season was over, and we had to turn in the jerseys. I stood in line and walked up to Coach Thomas, and he took Chuck's jersey and he asked me where my jersey was. I looked at him like he was crazy and said: *"You know where my jersey is. It is in the casket buried with Chuck."* Coach looked me in my face and told me that doesn't matter and that it's my problem and I need to pay for it. He gave me a week to pay the 60 dollars, or it will go on my record as a bill owed to the school. A level of rage boiled up in me toward Coach and Chuck. I instantly felt Big, Bad Chuck had all that mouth and muscle, yet he crumbled under the pressure of life and now I had to pay for his weakness. If the season wasn't over, I would have quit the team.

It's amazing how the smallest thing to one person both can and will have a lasting impression on others. You should never disregard someone's feelings. When I would reflect on my high school football career, I remember the camaraderie of the team and almost making it to the state. I also would remember that negative experience with Chuck and how everybody was building up this individual, yet he wasn't a nice person. In the yearbook was a big spread about him with his senior picture. I hated him and everything he stood for, and I hated everyone that built him and stood with him (which seemed like the whole school). I held onto that pain and anytime someone mentioned my high school football team, I would think about that situation and a sour feeling would flare up in my spirit. I would curse and be demeaning and think foul things about him.

Years later I was talking to a good friend of mine from high school. She was saying how wild it was to be out of high school for over 20 years. She was talking about her good times and being in the band and she mentioned me playing football. That anger flared up in my spirit and I started cursing and ranting and raving about Chuck and my experience. She stopped me, I can hear her calling my name: *"Elliott, Elliott you have to stop. I can understand that you're upset, but that was over 20 years ago. Chuck has been dead for over 25 years. You can't walk around with that much anger it will destroy you."* I took a minute, breathed, and I said yeah, you're right.

Romans 8:6 (NKJV) says *"to be carnally minded is death; but to be spiritually minded is life and peace."* To be carnally minded is to be controlled by the flesh which leads to death; death is separation from GOD. 1 Peter 5:8 (ESV) says *"Be sober minded; be watchful. Your adversary the devil prowls around like a roaring lion, seeking someone to devour."* Spewing hatred and curses is not of GOD. Those times when I dwelled in hate, I was being carnal minded and separating myself from the goodness of GOD. The devil wants to disrupt your life and your joy. I have since become aware of this key verse of scripture that made me rethink both my words and their impact: Psalm 16:24 (NIV)

"Gracious words are a honeycomb, sweet to the soul and healing to the bones."

It is amazing how I could release that burden that I had been carrying. It wasn't a constant burden, but it would show its face periodically: just enough to disrupt my peace. I don't know if it was my schoolmate's tone or just that fact that I valued and respected her to really listen and absorb what she had to say. GOD uses people to accomplish His goals: to pull us back to reality and into His Love. One thing is for certain GOD will meet you wherever you are. You just have to be willing to receive the message and allow the message to impact you. I didn't forgive fully that day, but the anger was gone. That night her words played over in my head and realized that I was over twice Chuck's age when he died. I thought about all the experiences I had in my life… all my joys and pains and my ups and downs I had that Chuck never fully experienced. Chuck never got the opportunity to live. I began to feel sorry for him. GOD began to work me.

Reflecting was my communion with the Father. You don't have to get on your knees to talk to the Father. He already knows how you're feeling, and He knows what you're thinking. He just wants you to express it to Him. In those moments I was appreciative of the life that God had given me. I wanted to be healed. I wasn't rejecting Him. He wants to be there for us, we just need to be aware of and acknowledge His presence in our everyday lives and our situations. Jesus said in Matthew 11:28-30 (NKJV): *"Come to me, all who labor and are heavy laden, and I will give you rest. Take my yoke upon you, and learn from me; for I am gentle and lowly in heart, and you will find rest for your souls. For my yoke is easy, and my burden is light."*

Give your pain, your heartache, your troubles, and your disappointments to Him and He will lighten your load. He gladly accepts them because He loves us. The problem is when either we don't fully submit, or we revisit the trial over and over again. Sometimes we think that we've dealt with it, but in reality, we have only taken the first steps. We think it is over because it's out of sight and out of mind. I have been guilty of this (I believe we all have been at some point). Misery loves company, true peace is a marathon and not a sprint. To receive peace, we must know God and to know God is to experience His love and know that just as He has forgiven the unthinkable for us, we must also forgive.

When I was presented with the opportunity to participate in this collaboration I thought about my situation, and I felt that it will be a great example of overcoming prolonged unforgiveness. It's been about 10 years since I had that conversation with my schoolmate and that I passed that anger and pain on. As I was writing my story that pain wanted to resurface, but I wouldn't let it. You have to control your life and not let your life control you. To tell my story, I had to relive the experience.

As I look through my spiritual eyes and reflect after having experienced more of life and having children of my own, I realized that he was just a kid. The devil convinced him that he had no choice. The devil will fill your head with negativity when there is seemingly no positivity present. Me, now being grown and having experienced numerous disappointments, I realized that the adults (his father, the coaches, his teachers and even the recruiter) in Chuck's life failed him. They left an emotional situation up to a person that hadn't learned how to deal with emotions. We all knew how important the Marines was to him.

The man in me wants to hug him and tell him that GOD loves him and tell him that life is full of peaks and valleys. I would tell him that he has a great life ahead of him that's full of people that love and believe in him. I would share that very few things work out how we want or expect them to. Like being on a boat, you have to ride the waves of life. With GOD and your faith in Him, you will always make it to the other side. He's not going to direct your path and then not let you reach your destination: even if you path involves playing a sport and shattering your ankle. When you trust and believe in Him, He will give you the desires of your heart. You make yourself so valuable that the Marines will beg you to be in the brotherhood. With a heart of forgiveness, I would show him love just like the great philosophers John Lennon and Paul McCartney who penned *"All You Need Is Love."*

"There is nothing you can do that can't be done…There's nowhere you can be that isn't where you're meant to be. It's easy. All you need is Love, all you need is love, all you need is love, love. Love is all you need."

To this point, I'll say: GOD is love. All you need is GOD. You can do anything, you can go anywhere, and you can accomplish everything. No evil can destroy you. No trial can defeat you. There is no pain on earth that love can't heal. No pain or unforgiveness can dwell in the presence of the Almighty GOD. All you need is GOD, GOD. GOD is all you need.

Sharing this part of my life's story blesses me knowing that there may be at least one person who can relate to holding on to prolonged pain and unforgiveness. Drawing closer to Him helps to keep me from being carnal minded and keeps my heart in check. The shirt I gave off my back no longer causes pain in my heart. I have let go and let God have His way.

E.T. Armstrong

"The Journey"

by E.T. Armstrong

Life can be troublesome at times
Though it's full of joy
And the love of GOD
It can and will become difficult
The trials of life
Can weigh you down
The spirit is delicate
And will be affected
By our experiences
By our choices
And many times, the choices of others
Will greatly affect us
Cause us
Pain
That will affect the spirit, heart and brain
The type of pain
That can remain for months or years
It will build
Create walls
Barriers that can't be easily broken
Hardening our hearts
For protection
Prevention
Of ever becoming that victim
To never be taken advantage of again
Sometimes you are
The perpetrator
The aggravator
The stimulator

Of your pain
Willingly or unwillingly
The outcome is the still the same
Pain
This anguish alters your view
Clouds your reality
Changes your mentality
This causes isolation
Isolation from others
Isolation from yourself
It changes your capacity
The ability
For love
Yes, it all goes back to love
Love is the foundation
The manifestation
Of all creation
GOD is Love
When you lose love
There is a separation
From the Father
And all that He intends for us
We lose ourselves from our full capacity
Of life, our purpose
We step on the treadmill of life
Running, but never reaching a destination
We jump on the hamster wheel running in circles
We get tired of carrying that burden
JESUS wants to take the weight
But you must take that first step
To relinquish
Release

That pain
You must forgive
Travel that road
To find yourself
The you the world needs
The one that GOD can use
To advance His kingdom
The road will be rocky and painful
You may want to turn back
Back to what you're accustomed to
The old, hurt you
But change is good
Stay the course
Walk in your strength
Step by step
and with every step
It will get easier
When you fully let go
You will see that the Lord
Was with you the whole time
Cheering you along
Only then will you fully live
When you open your heart to forgive

Elliott Armstrong

Elliott "E.T." Armstrong is a dreamer who has a vivid imagination and an animated way of telling a story. A native Carolinian, E.T. grew up alongside his younger sister. Though he had no brothers, he would find himself joining the brotherhood known as Kappa Alpha Psi during his college years. That process taught him much about perseverance and endurance, which are necessary in the Christian journey. To also help him along his journey, E.T. regularly listens to the teachings of Dr. Tony Evans and has recently signed up for his training center to increase his learning.

Professionally, he practices as a chiropractor and has been doing so for over 20 years. At a young age, E.T. would find himself having to recover from a motor vehicle accident that significantly impacted him. Chiropractic treatment became part of his recovery journey from injuries sustained. It would later become a motivation behind his career. As a former football player, he enjoys treating patients with sports injuries. He also takes joy in treating traumatic injuries to include auto accident and work related injuries. E.T. is dedicated to helping his patients achieve a pain free body.

E.T.'s creativity in thought was penned in his solo book published in the summer of 2012. "Pieces of a Man" is a compilation of over 200 pages of poems and short stories intended to stimulate the mind and pull on heart strings. Aside from becoming a published author and a practicing chiropractor who has been taking care of patients for over two decades, one of his greatest accomplishments is being a proud, devoted father. It is E.T.'s desire to become more and more like his Heavenly Father each day.

The Onion

Janice Bennett

Deciding to be a part of this project was a no brainer. The topic came to me readily. I had not counted the cost. I knew God wanted me to share and explore my experience with self-forgiveness. Not for me, but for you. The analogy of the onion lets you know that this journey has occurred in layers, and I'm not done yet. I want to be, but we're talking about a lifetime of choices, habits, pain, regret, remorse and shame. This commitment has required that I examine myself, remember my mistakes. The challenge is, how do I help someone else, when I am still being peeled back like an onion myself? I have come to learn that this onion thing is a lifelong process.

Truth, Isaiah 55:7 tells us Let the wicked forsake his way, and the unrighteous man his thoughts: and let him return unto the Lord, and He will have mercy upon him; and to our God, for he will abundantly pardon. Psalms 103 says, *"He does not treat us as our sins deserve or repay us according to our iniquities for as high as the heavens are above the earth, so great is His love for those who fear Him; as far as the east is from the west, so far has He removed our transgressions from us"*.

I wish I could tell you it is easy to know and apply this truth to my life. It wasn't. I had convinced myself and believed deceptively that salvation was all I could hope for. Hear me, His death, burial, and resurrection afforded you and I to live again with a clean slate. Despite what I know the Word says, my toughest hurdle has been myself. I believe His Word. The struggle has been believing it for me. Come with me as I share with you a few of the choices, mistakes, and misinformation that held me captive until I made the decision that His Word of forgiveness included me.

By the time I surrendered to Him as Lord of my life, I left behind, what I refer to, as *"roadkill."* That first layer of the onion being pulled back and discarded revealed so much pain, not for only me, but it exposed the shame I felt, for hurting those I loved the most. The peeling back was necessary so the bulk of the matter could be addressed. Self-forgiveness is not only about transgressions to others, but is also a deep dive that takes you back to where God reveals to you, the root of the matter. So, follow me as I share nakedly and no longer ashamed. Always remember, self-forgiveness will not ever happen until you are ready to see you. Allow the Spirit of the living God to be gentle with you, He knows when you're ready. I didn't say it would be easy, nor without pain. Afterall, the word of God says, *"it's good that I was afflicted that I might learn your precepts."* (Psalms 119:)

I was addicted to cocaine for 20 years. I lied, I stole, I manipulated, I was promiscuous: all as a result of my addiction. I hurt so many people and violated trust. When the Lord delivered me, I had to face life soberly. The pain that I self-medicated for had to be addressed. I had no idea why I chose the path I did. Those who loved me didn't understand either and this was perhaps the toughest place to begin my journey of self-forgiveness. The hurdles of their disappointment in me seem to add to the burden of forgiveness. If you're not careful, failure to forgive yourself can turn you into a people pleaser if it hasn't already. There is no freedom in that. Motives are really important in forgiveness, for others and yourself.

My mother transitioned to her heavenly home without witnessing what she believed God for. However, now that I have a better understanding of who Christ is in my life, it gives me a sort of peace, because I believe He showed her what would be. But even if she didn't see it, some of her last words to me were *"Janice, you're going to be okay."* I will work my way back from there.

My mom had been the most dependable of her siblings, though she was the youngest of nine. She made sure when time came that they all were properly buried and had headstones. Not grave markers, but granite headstones. Next to her brother, he transitioned after her, she is the only one without a headstone. Why? Because the insurance money that she left with me as beneficiary was spent on riotous living. I still have not rectified this matter. I've rationalized it, *"she's not there anyway."* My sister and I don't visit graves. My mother deserved no less than what she made sure everyone else had. Have I forgiven myself? Yes. Does recalling that time still elicit a tenderness? Yes. My shenanigans had my mother afraid to stay in her own home, because I had taken company with shady characters, and they threatened to blow up her home!!! Ouch! I had wounded the most precious, giving and forgiving person in my life, too many times to count. I stole from her. Not just tangibly, but her peace. She learned not to let me steal her joy. My apologies had become empty because, the reality was I wasn't sorry about what I had done, but I was sorry that I gotten caught. I've had to endure her crying uncontrollably over my behavior. It's that kind of hard truth that gets peeled back.

I had to learn to forgive myself for placing my sister in the position of having to take care of messes she didn't make. My self-forgiveness included confronting my life of hypocrisy, spiritually and naturally. Oh, I didn't tell you that the transgressions that I speak of, happened while I attended church and went to bible school. Perhaps you have experienced some of the same. Our paths may have been different, but we have all disappointed ourselves and those we care about and love. I decided that if I had to experience the pain, I was willing to let the Lord do the deep work. I would not and I still won't quit. The Bible says that *"the spirit of a man is the candle of the Lord"* (Proverbs 20:7). We have a conscience and how many times do we walk over it, ignore it? We created this place of loathing because we went against everything we know.

I had to forgive the woman who failed at marriage. I had to forgive the young woman who expected things from people that they did not have the capacity to give and calling it betrayal. I had to forgive her for treating the male relationships in her life as husbands and they were far from it. That girl was delusional. These are layers upon layers. But God was doing a deep work: the root of rejection, abandonment, low self-esteem, inferiority complex.

Now let's get to the best part. God in His infinite wisdom knew our end from our beginning. He is not, nor ever has He been shocked by our choices or behavior, good or bad. What He does is send these twins called *"grace and mercy."* They've been following us all the days of our lives. Consider the age-old adage of when you know better, you do better. If it's only intellectual knowledge, it's not so true. Our life experiences create pockets in our soul (our will, mind and emotions) that fill up with putrid lies that we tell ourselves, that are strongholds that we give the enemy bricks to build. There is no cure for this black hole except to flood it with the light of God's Word. I read a book once, entitled, *"Get Over Yourself"* by Rev Dr. James Love. God used it as a tool to help me understand that the reality of it all, was that I was exercising false humility, though I didn't say it out loud, I wanted people to understand how sorry I was for it all. Truth of the matter, who am I to suggest that I could pay a price as costly as my Savior Jesus Christ? Who was I to think that His shed blood had power for everything else but not me. How pompous! Now the inside work was necessary, I had to yield to the Potter's hands. It didn't feel good. I was gracefully broken a few times so that He could continue His work. *"For we are His workmanship, created in Christ Jesus for good works, which God prepared beforehand that we should walk in them."* I am glad He saw way past my faults and saw needs. When the weeds of unforgiveness for myself arise, because they do, I am better equipped and I know better, so I cast down that imagination and bring every thought captive and every high thing that exalts itself against the knowledge of God. (2 Corinthians 10:5-6) Great is His faithfulness unto us! Be free, live free!

Janice Bennett

Elder Janice Bennett is a native of Washington, DC. She is the youngest daughter born to Ray and Juanita Bennett. Elder Janice received her education in both the parochial and DC public school system. She has been a registered nurse for 41 years and she relocated to Houston Texas where she is currently Director of Nursing for a hospice provider.

Elder Janice is a graduate of Calvary Bible Institute. and wants to pursue her Bachelors Degree in Biblical Studies and Pastoral Leadership.

She was raised in the admonition of the Lord but wandered for over 20 years in the wilderness of disobedience and addiction. She rededicated her life to Christ in 1993 and continued to live a life or carnality until her complete surrender to our Lord and Savior in 2007. God has done a quick work, and she was ordained to the ministry in 2010.

She is a member of Jesus Christ Holiness Church where she actively serves in ministry. God has entrusted her with Withered Hand Ministry. A ministry dedicated to those who want to do and be all that the Lord has called them to but find themselves "stuck" as she once was. She sits under and submits to the authority and leadership of Pastor Laquantus Broussard.

Elder Janice has a love for the lost, the bound, and the brokenhearted. One of her most favorite scriptures is 1 Timothy 1: 15-16 "The saying is sure and worthy of full acceptance, that Christ Jesus came into the world to save sinners—of whom I am the foremost. But for that very reason I received mercy, so that in me, as the foremost, Jesus Christ might display the utmost patience, making me an example to those who would come to believe in him for eternal life."

Elder Janice often says and believes she went through, so you don't have to……

Apology Denied, Forgiveness Applied

LaKesha L. Williams

Often times when we think of forgiveness, we immediately think of receiving an apology and then forgiveness follows. Many of us think of forgiveness as an "if-then action," if you apologize then I will forgive you BUT if that is something we live by does that mean if we don't receive an apology then forgiveness never takes place? Leaves a lot to ponder right? When Jesus died on the Cross, He died for the forgiveness of our sins, but did we ever give Him an apology before He so willingly laid down His life? What if that was His prerequisite, none of us would be saved right now and Jesus was blameless.

Where am I going with this? I am glad you asked, I just wanted to share my story and journey to forgiveness and what that looks like when an apology is denied but forgiveness must still be applied.

I believe everything that both has happened and will happen to me has an intended purpose, and I must discover that purpose. In my childhood, I was raped by one male and molested by five males, and one female. For more than half my life I walked around with a sign on my chest that said, VICTIM. I was in bondage to the emotional, physical, and spiritual scars that can come from being raped and molested at a young age. These scars made me a victim twice, once in my childhood and again in my adulthood, when I had to confront these sexual traumas.

The opposite of a victim is a victor. Merriam-Webster defines a victim as one that is subjected to oppression, hardship, or mistreatment. Merriam-Webster defines victor as a person who defeats an enemy or opponent in a battle, game, or other competition; so, it follows that victory is defined as an act of defeating an enemy or opponent in a battle, game, or other competition. I Corinthians 15:57 says, ... *"but thanks be to God, who gives us the victory [as conquerors] through our Lord Jesus Christ"*.

In 1988, my family and I moved from North Carolina to Temple Hills, Maryland. We lived in an apartment in Maryland off St. Barnabas Road behind a bowling alley. I was five years old when I was raped by a boy who was three years older than me. I don't recall the time of year the rape took place, but I can clearly remember that horrific day. My life would forever be changed. The events and incidents that followed created a crescendo of sexual trauma that reverberated into my adult years.

I lived with my mom, dad, and older brother. I often went outside with my brother and played with his friends' younger siblings. I don't recall if it was a school day, but I do remember it was warm enough for kids to be outside playing. All the neighborhood kids loved to get together and play a big game of hide-and-go-seek. When there were too many kids, we'd hide in pairs, so the game wouldn't be so hard and wouldn't go on forever. We had no method of choosing partners other than picking whoever was nearest to us. I just happened to be near a boy who was my brother's friend and lived in my neighborhood. He was light-skinned with freckles, red hair, and thick red lips. He grabbed my arm, and we ran into the woods behind the apartments along with the other children and their partners to find a good hiding spot.

I remember his hand was sticky and damp with sweat. He ran with my forearm in his hand the whole time, basically pulling me along. We ran deep into the woods for a while because my legs were tired, my arm hurt from his grip, and the screams of the other children were distant. Finally, we stopped running and I rested against a nearby tree. I was tired but still caught up in the excitement of playing hide-and-go-seek, one of my favorite games to play. The thrill of wondering if I would be found or winning the game was all I could think about. Usually when we would play, I'd never win because I wasn't a good hider. This day, I believed that since we had run so far, we would win, but little did I know my partner had other plans for me. Thinking back, I believe his intentions were premeditated.

After I caught my breath, I asked myself where exactly we were supposed to be hiding, because it seemed like we were just standing behind trees, which wasn't a good hiding spot in my five-year-old opinion. I wasn't really paying attention to him, instead I was looking back. I don't remember what he was doing, but when I turned to see where he was, he was right in my face. He was standing so close to me. He put both hands on the tree around me and pressed himself into me, pressing me hard against the tree. I can still remember the cold hard tree against my back.

At this point, he was so close that his lips were almost touching mine and I could feel his hot breath on my face. He was breathing hard and slowly. I felt like I was going to suffocate from his weight and from the funk of his breath that smelled like old hotdogs and underarm pits. As I turned my face away to try and get some fresh air, he grabbed my face and tried to kiss me. I held my lips tightly together in disgust, but I felt his tongue trying to force its way into my mouth followed by teeth and saliva.

I can't recall what happened between the nasty kiss and what came next, but I do remember noticing that we were standing by a ravine that I hadn't noticed before. There was a slight drop with a stream of water at the bottom. I remember him standing behind me holding both my arms and saying in a low husky voice, "If you scream, I will throw you down there and the alligators will eat you." I felt his breath and his lips touch my right ear as he talked. I was terrified and all I could think about was the alligators eating me. I was paralyzed with fear. He said, "Do everything I say do." He was taller and bigger than me, so I agreed. Something inside of me said, RUN, but my legs would not work. All I could think about was the alligators. I did everything he said, and I didn't scream. He laid a jacket on the ground. To this day I don't remember either of us having a jacket on or where he got the jacket from. He told me to lay on the jacket on my stomach. I was scared so I did as I was told.

The ground was cool and hard. I remember hearing leaves crunching so maybe it was fall. I also recall the smell of dirt as I laid there. He straddled me from behind and began grinding himself against me. I felt like I couldn't breathe from his weight and at this point, the side of my face was in the dirt. I felt his breath on my neck and felt him lick and kiss the back of my neck a couple of times. After an immeasurable amount of time, I felt him stop; I didn't know then what he was doing, but I know now he was unbuttoning his pants because next, he pulled my pants and underwear down. I just remember laying there still, quiet, and scared. I didn't know what was happening.

I was still lying flat on my stomach as he positioned himself, this time with our skin touching and his penis grinding against my bottom. I was unaware then, but now I know he wasn't quite sure what to do because it took him some time to figure it out, but once he was erect, he was able to penetrate me anally, at which point, I felt pressure, pain and then I blacked out. I don't know how long this act lasted or when it ended, but my memory picks back up as we were walking through the woods back home. There were no other kids around and it seemed late in the day because it was getting dark outside. He walked me back to the edge of the woods where he reminded me of what he would do to me (throw me in the ravine with the alligators) if I told anyone. He left me standing there and ran off to do whatever. I slowly walked back to my building where I was met by my mother, who was furious because she had been looking for me. It was around 6:00 p.m. when my dad got off work and because I was missing, she was late picking him up. I remember being scolded and shuffled into the car, so I never had a chance to tell my mom what happened. For years it was like having a red stain on a white shirt that constantly stayed in my memory. When I decided to write about it, the enemy tried to make me believe it didn't happen or that it was made up. But the pain I remember was very real and the effects of the trauma were even more real. That day is so imprinted in my mind.

I can't remember how long we stayed in that apartment complex, but I do remember it wasn't long before we moved into a house. After the rape, I never remember seeing him ever again. Or, it could have been that I never went outside to play again. It was difficult to remember much after that day. I think the rape is the last memory I have of living at the apartment. I do have the memory of almost drowning at the complex's swimming pool. I remember the day I went missing when I tried to walk to my mother's friend's house, but I don't know if those instances came before or after the rape.

We moved to a house in Temple Hills. My mother would sometimes send my brother and I out of town to stay with relatives for spring break and sometimes a week of summer break. The molestations happened during this time and lasted over about four years between ages five and nine. I remember the ages because I recall the incidents started after the rape and continued until my little sister was born in 1992, when I was nine. That is also when my mom stopped sending us to North Carolina during school breaks. Although I can't remember the order when they occurred, I do remember the incidents well.

The first incident I remember was with my father's uncle. I recall my great uncle and I were sitting in a pickup truck in a field. He unzipped his pants and pulled his penis out. This is the first time I remember seeing an actual penis. I don't recall exactly how old I was. He wanted me to touch it. I didn't want to touch it. I thought I would hurt him if I touched it. He wasn't erect and since he was an old man, it looked weird just lying there, and I didn't want to touch it. I remember him grabbing my hand to guide me to touch him, but I kept pulling my hand back. He got upset and said I would get in trouble if I didn't touch it, so I touched it. He said, "See you're not hurting me." I just remember holding my hand on it. He said, "Rub it." So, I did, but nothing really happened. After I rubbed it, he put it away and we went back to the house. This was a one-time event. I never told anyone, and I don't remember feeling any emotion. However, I do remember wondering what other penises looked like. My father's uncle passed away when I was young.

On another occasion, I was molested by a female relative. She wanted to see what my breasts looked like, and she wanted to know if I had pubic hair. This happened as we were changing for bed. That night we both slept in the same bed. I remember her asking if I had ever kissed anyone. I said, "No." She suggested I try it with her. Again, I held my lips tight together because it was a nasty experience. After the kiss I am not sure exactly what happened next or how we got to where we did, but I was laying on my back and she was on top of me in the missionary position. She was trying to grind in between my legs. I remember lying there unsure of what was going on. After a little while, she stopped and lay next to me. She said, "Did that feel good?" I said, "No. I didn't feel anything." She sighed, rolled over, and went to sleep. I just laid there for a while. I don't remember going to sleep. I didn't say, "Stop!" I didn't scream for help. I just did what she told me to do, though I sensed it was wrong. I never told anyone about that either (although she never threatened me not to tell), and it never happened with her again.

I was later molested repeatedly by a male relative I refer to as the primary molester. Those dirty experiences included everything from touching my privates with clothes on and off, fingering, dry-humping, and me performing oral sex. This went on for years at so many different occasions. Sometimes it would happen multiple times a day, morning, noon, and night. These instances never included penetration. They were so frequent that I just expected it to happen and did what he asked of me. His favorite thing was touching my privates and then having me perform oral sex on him. He taught me how to do it right, not scrape him with my teeth, slow down, and focus. One time he invited one of his friends to touch me. He touched my breast and dry humped me for a little while before the primary molester stopped him. That same day, another friend of his came by, and the primary molester told me to go in the closet with his friend. He touched my privates, and I gave him a hand job. When we were done, he left me in the closet. I could hear them both in the room, but I was left in the closet for hours. They finally let me out before any adults came home.

Whenever I saw this male relative, he would touch me, or I would perform oral sex on him. That was the "norm." I grew used to it. He never threatened me, but he did say that it was "our little secret", and I couldn't tell anyone else about it or he would get in trouble. So, I never told anyone. For a long time, I felt guilty about it because I let it go on for so long, and I knew it wasn't right. I knew because he would always remind me that it was a secret. I never really felt anything during those times. I couldn't understand how he seemed to feel pleasure from something I felt nothing from.

The last molester from my childhood was my uncle's girlfriend's son. Like the others, he was older than me. My family and I had come for a visit and stayed with my uncle and his family. One night my uncle's girlfriend cooked spaghetti. I don't remember eating any. Everyone who ate some got food poisoning and had to go to the hospital. Her son, my drunk uncle, and I were left at the house while everyone else went to the hospital. My uncle was in bed. The son and I were in the living room watching TV. He wanted us to go into his room. We went into his room, and I sat on the bed. He asked if I wanted to see his penis. I was unsure, and I started to feel kind of afraid. I got up to go to the door. He got up, locked the door, and stood in front of it. He pressed me against the wall facing him. He told me to pull my pants down. It was dark in the room except for the light from a small lamp on the nightstand. I pulled my pants down, he also pulled his down. He came up to me, and I could see that his penis was curved. He tried to penetrate me while I was standing against the wall. His penis felt hard. I told him I didn't want to. He said it wouldn't hurt and it wouldn't take long. I was afraid, so I asked if we could do something else hoping he would stop trying to do whatever he was trying to do. He agreed. I was relieved until he threatened me. He said he would kill me if I told anyone. I pulled my pants up. He told me to go sit on the bed. I sat on the side of the bed as he laid down on the bed with his pants off. He asked me to put my mouth on his penis and he would let me go afterwards. He said I had to do it for at least one minute. There was a clock in the room, and I watched the clock as I performed oral sex on him. When one minute was up, I ran out of the room to the room I was staying in and never came back out for the rest of the night. For a couple days after that I had a dry ring around my mouth that was itchy and irritating. I remember feeling dumb afterwards. But, other than the first time when I was raped, with him was the only time I felt fear. I was afraid because I thought he would really hurt me if I didn't do what he said, and if he stuck his curved penis in me. He has been incarcerated for many years since then, though it is possible I was not his first victim. Prior to my uncle dating his mom, it was rumored that her daughter was removed from her custody due to allegations of rape and molestation. The only time I had experienced penetration was in my behind when I was raped the first time. I remembered that pain.

There was one other incident with him where he was caught by my mom with his hand on my private area. I was the only one who got in trouble. That was the last time I remember something happening with him. Sometimes, I think about what I could have done differently. What if I had told someone as soon as it happened? What if I fought? What if I said, "No"? For many years I carried a lot of guilt, shame, and embarrassment surrounding these sufferings I've just shared from my childhood. It was not easy sharing them, but I know they needed to be shared because I am not the only person who has experienced childhood sexual abuse (CSA).

****

I think it's important that I stop and talk about CSA, as a trained sexual assault victim advocate, I cannot pass up an opportunity to educate.

CSA is a significant public health problem and an adverse childhood experience (ACE). CSA refers to the involvement of a child (person less than 18 years old) in sexual activity that violates the laws or social taboos of society and that he/she:

- does not fully comprehend;
- does not consent to or is unable to give informed consent to, or
- is not developmentally prepared for and cannot give consent to.

Many children wait to report or never report child sexual abuse. Therefore, the numbers below likely underestimate the true impact of the problem. Although estimates vary across studies, the research shows:

- About 1 in 4 girls and 1 in 13 boys in the United States experience child sexual abuse.
- Someone known and trusted by the child or child's family members perpetrates 91% of child sexual abuse.
- The total lifetime economic burden of child sexual abuse in the United States in 2015 was estimated to be at least $9.3 billion.

Experiencing child sexual abuse can affect how a person thinks, acts, and feels over a lifetime. This can result in short-term and long-term physical, mental, and behavioral health consequences.

Examples of physical health consequences include:

- sexually transmitted infections (STIs)
- physical injuries
- chronic conditions later in life, such as heart disease, obesity, and cancer

Examples of mental health consequences include:

- depression
- posttraumatic stress disorder (PTSD) symptoms

Examples of behavioral consequences include:

- substance use/misuse, including opioid misuse.

- risky sexual behaviors, meaning sex with multiple partners or behaviors that could result in pregnancy or STIs.
- increased risk for perpetration of sexual violence.
- increased risk for suicide or suicide attempts

Experiencing child sexual abuse can also increase a person's risk for future victimization. For example, recent studies have found:

- Females exposed to child sexual abuse are at 2-13 times increased risk of sexual violence victimization in adulthood.
- People who experienced child sexual abuse are at twice the risk for non-sexual intimate partner violence.

Adults are responsible for ensuring that children have safe, stable, nurturing relationships and environments. Resources for CSA have mostly focused on treatment for victims and criminal justice-oriented approaches for perpetrators. These efforts are important after child sexual abuse has occurred. However, little investment has been made in primary prevention or preventing child sexual abuse. Effective evidence-based strategies are available to proactively protecting children from child sexual abuse, but few have been widely disseminated. More resources are needed to develop, evaluate, and implement evidence-based CSA primary prevention strategies. These strategies can help ensure that all children have safe, stable, nurturing relationships and environments.

Credit: https://www.cdc.gov/violenceprevention/childsexualabuse/fastfact.html

I tried so many times to erase these memories from my mind and pretend like it didn't happen, and I was successful until high school when it seemed everyone was having sex. By this time, I had realized exactly what happened when I was raped, and if that was what sex was like I wanted no parts of it. All I could do was associate sex with pain. So, I decided I would never have sex, because I never wanted to experience pain like I'd experienced that day. I was terrified of sex and the thought of sex made me very uncomfortable. For years, I associated rape with sex until a close friend of mine clarified. What happened to me when I was raped and molested was not sex, it was assault and abuse, and I shouldn't compare the two. That conversation was freeing and shifted my perspective.

Oftentimes, that is exactly what we need, a perspective shift and this is the very reason I've chosen to share these stories with you. Not so you can feel pity for me or say OMG I am so sorry that happened to you. No! I've shared these stories because no matter what the action was that was committed against you, forgiveness is a requirement not an option.

Forgiveness will lead to victory even if there is never an apology or acknowledgement of the wrongdoing that happened to you. Again, forgiveness is a requirement not an option. Matthew 6:14-15 says, *"For if you forgive others their trespasses [their reckless and willful sins], your heavenly Father will also forgive you. But if you do not forgive others [nurturing your hurt and anger with the result that it interferes with your relationship with God], then your Father will not forgive your trespasses."*

Nowhere in Matthew 6:14-15 does it say, *"After you have received and accepted an apology, forgive others their trespasses."* How often are we denied the apology we feel like we so desperately need. None of my molesters nor my rapist came and apologized to me or even acknowledged their wrong doings.

You may not have been raped, molested or sexually assaulted, but my question to you is, what embodies the spirit that we call our offender? It is really about all those who've offended you and everyone who knew who didn't say anything? This may not have been your experience but replace my offender with the person who offended you and choose to apply forgiveness even when an apology has been denied.

LaKesha L. Williams

Affectionately known as Coach Kesha, LaKesha L. Williams is a mastermind in her own right. She is a world-renowned author, acclaimed speaker, publisher, and Minister of the Gospel of Jesus Christ. This dynamic strategic visionary is the CEO and owner of The VTF Group LLC and The VTF Publishing House, a business consulting firm and top-notch hybrid publishing house that is known for multiple national and international best-sellers.

LaKesha has authored twenty books, including multiple bestsellers. Her most recent project, Unquestionably Free was released February of 2023. LaKesha is also the Founder of Unquestionably Free Global Ministries, a ministry of hope, love, restoration and freedom.

LaKesha is a board-certified master mental health coach, a certified professional Christian life coach, and a trained sexual assault victim advocate. As a virgin in her early 40's, LaKesha is an advocate of abstinence, purity, and virginity until marriage.

LaKesha enjoys serving in the community. When she is not serving or working in the community, LaKesha can be found spending time with her family and close friends, watching movies, sharing laughs, trying new recipes, traveling, and creating new memories.

For bookings, business, and ministry inquiries, please email info@coachkesha.com

Conclusion

You have probably heard the saying: *"Why do bad things happen to good people?"* The harsh reality is we all go through some type of suffering: some of it is a product of our choices and some of it is a product of someone else's choices. All of it is either God-arranged or God-allowed as one late pastor used to say. For some of the bad choices of others that have negatively impacted our lives, we may find that we won't receive an apology. We may find that our name gets dragged for something someone else has done. We may get dismissed even after giving the shirts off our backs. Sometimes the ones who are supposed to protect us are the ones who bring harm to us. These circumstances are far too common. I am led to remind you of a thing:

"He was despised and rejected by men,
A Man of sorrows and pain and acquainted with grief;
And like One from whom men hide their faces
He was despised, and we did not appreciate His worth or esteem Him.

But He was wounded for our transgressions,
He was crushed for our wickedness [our sin, our injustice, our wrongdoing];

The punishment [required] for our well-being fell on Him,
And by His stripes (wounds) we are healed."
Isaiah 53:4-5 (AMP)

When Jesus went through the worst of it all for something He did not do, He didn't take on the weight of lack of forgiveness.

He did take the weight of our sins on the cross He had to carry, in every lash He took, and through the blood He shed. Lest we forget!

Appendix A

Forgiveness Quotes

Forgiveness is the foundation to your spiritual house. Without it you will have trouble withstanding the storms of life. – E.T. Armstrong

Forgiving is like being in AA or NA: you have to take it one day at a time. – E.T. Armstrong

Forgiving the people you rely on is difficult because we see them as super human, but in reality they're just human. – E.T. Armstrong

If you fail to forgive, you fail to be forgiven. – Danielle N. Hall

The heart is a container that if in it fond memories are kept, it does the body well. – Danielle N. Hall

Lack of forgiveness is like having on fetters and shackles: it hinders progress. – Danielle N. Hall

A major release happens when the mouth speaks and the heart is in harmony to forgive. – Danielle N. Hall

When you forgive, you take the weight off of your shoulders, the strain off of your heart, and the shackles off of your feet. – Danielle N. Hall

Songs of Healing & Forgiveness

A Heart That Forgives by Kevin LeVar
Broken by Shekinah Glory Ministry
Broken But I'm Healed by Byron Cage
Give Me A Clean Heart by Fred Hammond
Healed by Donald Lawrence
Healer by Isabel Davis
Healer by Ntokozo Mbambo
Healer by Trent Cory
Healer by William Murphy
Healer of My Emotions by Damien Sneed
Healing by Kelly Price
Healing Power by Xolly McWango
Healing Stream/We Wait On You by Judith Christie McAllister
Journal by Casey J.
Mender by Richard Smallwood
Mend Me by Kristen Hicks
Necessary by Dennis Reed & GAP
Surgery by Testament & L. Spenser Smith
Teach Me by L. Spencer Smith
The Curse Is Broken by Todd Galberth

About the Author

Danielle N. Hall is a Board Certified Christian Counselor and Mental Health Coach who is an advocate for all to recognize and achieve their divine purpose. Additionally, is a licensed minister who is continually looking for ways to enlighten, to encourage, and to empower others through this journey called life.

She is a sexual abuse survivor and the visionary/founder of V.O.I.C.E. (Victorious Overcomers Inspiring Christian Empowerment) which is a ministry that services women who have been sexually assaulted or abused. She is the sole author of her debut book "Dew Drops: Refreshing for the Soul", her sophomore book: Amazon #1 Bestseller "Dirty Little Secrets & The Little White Lie." and her junior release: Grace to Endure: You Don't Know My Story". Danielle has been a contributing author of 5 projects: She Wouldn't Let Me Fall (2018), Hope for the Overcomers Soul (2018), My Whole Self Matters Empowerment Journey Journal (2019), My Praise Is My Weapon (2020) and God Blocked It (2023).

She is a budding entrepreneur and is the owner of both SOL by Danielle (a greeting card service launched in 2017) and The Butterfly Effect by Danielle (a butterfly themed jewelry company launched in August 2019). In May 2023, Danielle launched The R.O.P.E., LLC (The Realm of Possibility Experience) where she will employ her skillset as a coach and counselor. She is a recently widowed mother of 3, who endeavors to both achieve and maintain balance given the demands of family, work, ministry, and self.

Other books by the Author

Dew Drops: Refreshing for the Soul (Author)
Dirty Little Secrets & The Little White Lie (Author)
Grace to Endure: You Don't Know My Story (Author)
She Wouldn't Let Me Fall (Contributing Author)
God Blocked It (Contributing Author)
My Whole Self Matters Empowerment Journey Journal (Contributing Author)
My Praise is My Weapon (Contributing Author)
Hope for the Overcomers Soul (Contributing Author)

About the Publisher

We believe that publishing a book is about more than becoming an author. It is about bringing a vision to fruition, building an audience, and expanding one's influence. The VTF Group LLC offers a variety of publishing options.

The VTF Group has earned its positive reputation because we go out of our way to deliver truly exceptional service to each of our customers, something we like to call "The White Glove Experience." Not all publishers are created equal, and we know that when extra attention is needed, our "White Glove Experience" will not disappoint. As an experienced team of authors, we also specialize in coaching you through the publishing process to bring your vision to fruition.

Contact us today via www.TheVTFGroup.com to schedule a free 15-minute consultation.

www.ingramcontent.com/pod-product-compliance
Lightning Source LLC
Chambersburg PA
CBHW071225160426
43196CB00012B/2417